Advance Praise *for* MOMENTUM

"Brent is one of the most dynamic real estate speakers and trainers in the world today. His ideas, strategies, and wisdom inspire his audiences ... but more importantly, he changes your paradigm and your paycheck! He shows you not only how to make more money ... but reminds you with his passion and humor just how fun the game of life is!"

Curtis Johnson
Wall Street Journal's Top 50 Real Estate Teams in America

"Brent Gove is one of the most inspiring individuals I have ever met in my life! He's one of my favorite speakers in real estate today."

Jay Kinder
Wall Street Journal's Top 50 Agents Worldwide

"Brent Gove is the most energetic, sharing, and caring professional coach and trainer that I have ever heard! His passion is contagious! It's an honor to know him. Thank you!"

Tom Daves
Wall Street Journal's #7 Ranked Realtor in the United States

"It's been almost two years since I was coached by Brent Gove. He was instrumental in jumpstarting my career during a time when so many agents left the business. Since then I've been cranking it out! I've been elected to the board of my local association and will serve as its president in 2013! Whenever colleagues ask me how I've been able to thrive in such a difficult market, I point them right at Brent. Each day I say 'thank you' for all Brent's help and mentoring! My life and career has been blessed and I thank God for allowing our paths to cross."

Shari Aguilar
Grupe Real Estate

BRENT GOVE

MOMENTUM
MOMENTUM
MOMENTUM
MOMENTUM
MOMENTUM

A STRATEGIC GUIDE TO SUCCESS FOR REAL ESTATE AGENTS AND BROKERS

IRISH
CANON
PRESS

BERKELEY·CALIFORNIA

Momentum: A Strategic Guide to Success for
Real Estate Agents and Brokers

Copyright © 2011 by Brent Gove

IRISH
CAΠOΠ
PRESS

For sales, bulk discounts, or further information please contact:
Irish Canon Press, LLC
2625 Alcatraz Avenue Ste. #105
Berkeley, CA 94705
info@IrishCanonPress.com
www.IrishCanonPress.com

To hire Brent Gove to speak at your event, to order DVDs, or to get a schedule of his seminar dates and locations, contact Brent's office at BrentGoveSeminars.com or (916) 223-5555

Brent has a newsletter! For more information, go to
www.BrentGove.com or www.BrentGoveSeminars.com

Brent is on Twitter: @GoveMomentum
Follow Brent, Momentum, and Irish Canon Press on Facebook

Cover design by Hans Bennewitz

Interior design by Williams Writing, Editing & Design

Publisher's Cataloging-in-Publication Data

Gove, Brent.
Momentum : a strategic guide to success for real
estate agents and brokers / by Brent Gove.
p. cm.
ISBN 978-0-615-38665-2

1. Real estate business. 2. Real estate agents.
3. House selling. I. Title.

HD1375 .G68 2011
333.33 --dc22   2011929481

IMPORTANT NOTE

To My Loving Wife Kathy *and* Our Five Beautiful Children:
You inspire me! Thank you for loving me unconditionally.

Contents

Acknowledgments

The Lord, who has blessed my life abundantly. To my children, Kristina, Dillon, Sarah, Megan, and Ty. My parents, Jim and Carol Gove. Randy and Melissa Gove. My sister, Darcie, and her husband, Mike Lenno. My pastor . . . Francis Anfuso. James and Jennie Stroup, Barry and Anita Mathis; true friends. Ray and Sondra Jensen, Robert Lewis, Craig Proctor, Brian Buffini, Coach Ken, Bob Corcoran, Howard Brinton, Jeff and Marcee Wilhems, Jay Kinder, Michael Reese, Tim Yee, Gary Keller, Mo Anderson, Mark Willis, and Mary Tennant, Rick and Maureen Barker, Curtis Johnson, Matt Wagner, Danny Griffin, Brian Moses, Daniel Pendley, Joe Stump, Mike Ferry, Tom Ferry, Pastor Bob Hasty, Pastor Frank Colacurcio, Pastor John Houghton, Dr. Lance Wallnau, Bob Hartley, Dr. Denis Waitley, Skip Ross, Zig Ziglar, and coach Gary Summerhays.

Special thanks: To my publisher at Irish Canon Press, Sean Harvey, I extend my heartfelt gratitude for helping me realize this dream. He believed in me, supported me, and brought out the best I have to offer here. Without him, this book would not have been possible.

MOMENTUM

MOMENTUM

MOMENTUM

MOMENTUM

MOMENTUM

Introduction

I'm going tell you about a conversation that changed me: Many years ago at one of my very first conferences I was speaking with someone — an expert in real estate — and this highly successful agent was kind enough to pull me aside and share some of his methods with me. I didn't actually know this agent very well, but nonetheless he dove right in and began to tell me his secrets. I thought I was being polite, and for each idea that came out of his mouth, I was nodding approval, but ... honestly? Everything he said just bounced off me.

When I look back now, I can *clearly* remember that for each point he made I quickly thought, "That won't work ..." or "I would never do that ..."

Nope. He couldn't get through to me!

Here this agent was sharing his business secrets with me, but I was young and stubborn and I realize now that I was covered from head to toe in a suit of armor. Yep! *Ping ... ping ... ping* ... each new idea and concept just bounced off my idea-proof metal suit.

So why wasn't I listening?

I wasn't listening because this agent didn't do things the way that I did them. I had just sold six houses in the previous month and I felt like a king. And the fact is that other than "my way" and how I'd been trained, I'd never even really considered that there were other methods out there.

This was real estate. Real estate is simple, right? One ... two ... three ... You get a little training and then you work hard and then you make lots of money.

Looking back, I realize now that my resistance to his methods wasn't about me knowing it all. Nor was it even about me knowing more than he did. The truth is that his ideas and methods were so out-of-the-box and so unfamiliar to me that I felt

3

threatened. I didn't know you could do the things he was doing. What's more, as I look back I realize that I was a little worried that if this agent was doing things that *really* worked — but which I had never even heard of — then it was also quite possible that I was doing something wrong.

Of course, I now know that it wasn't *my* methods that were wrong. Not at all. It was my reaction to *his* methods that was backwards.

As far as my real estate business goes, that day marked the very end of my phase of wrong-headed thinking. As I walked away from the agent I was struck — like a piano dropping right down on my head from a third-story window — by something that has served me better than all the information contained in 500 real estate books *combined*. I walked away from that conversation with the realization that I was not open to learning. Furthermore, I realized that, in the long run, being closed off to new ideas was not going to be good for me or good for my business.

That realization both seriously challenged *and* changed me. Because if I hadn't become aware of my own subconscious resistance to learning, I wouldn't be in real estate today (and I certainly wouldn't have enjoyed the success that I've had).

To repeat: with all the changes and challenges that the real estate business has undergone over the years, if I had remained closed off to learning then I wouldn't be in real estate today.

Not a chance.

If you've been in real estate for any length of time, I'll bet you know an agent who is doing pretty well right now. On the flip side, I'm also willing to make the bet that you know some agents that have recently left real estate.

In short, you know agents who have been forced out.

A lot of people in our industry are struggling to survive the transition from bull to bear market. I see it every day with agents that I have known for years. Nationally, the worst markets are experiencing extreme price deflation, and most of the rest of the country is, at best, experiencing flat-lining stagnation.

Struggling in your chosen profession isn't anyone's idea of fun. But if you are still in the game, even if you are struggling, it's not too late to turn it all around.

In regard to real estate and *Momentum* and what you're about to read, I won't lie to you and make outrageous promises. I won't tell you that just reading *Momentum* will guarantee that you'll make more money than you've ever dreamed. We all know that there are lots of other books out there that promise you incredible success.

I can't do that.

What's more, you'll have to decide for yourself just how much those "promises" and "guarantees" are actually worth.

I *will* promise you that to survive and thrive in real estate in the 21st century you are going to have to be flexible. To be successful I can guarantee that you're going to have to be open to learning and change and growth.

And that means that if you've been doing things the same way for a while, you're going to have to adapt. Whether you're just trying to survive, or whether you're fortunate enough to be on cruise control, at some point you're going to have to change your wardrobe. That means you need new ideas to stay ahead of the competition. This means you have to be open to learning.

I don't care how much experience you have, or how successful you are, in the new economy, wearing idea-proof suits of armor is not only poor fashion sense, it's just plain bad business.

But let's look at it differently. Change? Learning? Improvement? What on earth could be wrong with any of that? Growth and knowledge? These are *all* fantastic things! These things *not only* set you apart, they help you thrive.

But some people have to have guarantees. I know I love 'em. So I'll give you two: first, if you are an agent who is closed off to learning, then you are in big trouble. In short, closed off?

You probably will not survive in this business. Second, on the flip side, if you are an agent who is open to learning, then you can absolutely achieve great success in *any* real estate market.

That's *any* market.

And my experience has shown me that it's really no more complicated than that. By making a few changes to your business model, even a tough economy could represent the greatest achievement of your professional life. That's right! I said it. This could be the time in your career when you learn that you have what it takes to succeed in any market.

While that's a powerful statement, it's an even more powerful feeling. Because, as someone once said, life is not about waiting for the storms to pass, it's about learning to dance in the rain.

If you're willing to implement the methods presented here in *Momentum* then you can drastically improve your business and make more money. But first, you've got to take off your suit of armor. And for those of you who have been doing things the same way for a long, long time, you know *exactly* what I mean. To clarify, with few exceptions, if you haven't changed your business model (perhaps drastically) in the last five years, I'd be very surprised if your income hasn't fallen off. Because just treading water until the appearance of the next superbubble isn't going to work this time. You've got to be willing to look at your business in a new way. Growth and change are hard, but they are also incredibly rewarding, and you've got to be willing to get a little bit uncomfortable to make the necessary changes and thrive.

I'm here to help. Don't wait for the piano to fall on your head. (Talk about discomfort!) I'm here to walk you through the door to your professional future.

I'm passionate about coaching and real estate success and I love what I do. *I love it!* And thankfully, I'm good at it. I wrote *Momentum* to help you see that there are new and different ways to do many of the things you probably take for granted (or ignore completely). Simple time-savers, new ways to look at old problems, quick fixes and long-term solutions — along with hiring staff, teams of agents, working with buyers, working with sellers, and open houses — are all here in the pages of *Momentum*.

So, if you're wearing one, take off that suit of armor. Being able to "change" and getting "uncomfortable" are strengths, not weaknesses. The strong adapt. The best business people make changes and thrive.

I very much want you to thrive.

And if you are the type of person who makes it a point to be open to learning, then good for you! Because adopting the methods outlined in *Momentum* will help you become a better agent.

And *nothing* would please me more.

ONE

ONE

ONE

ONE

How Buyers Are the Gift of Gold

I have a confession to make: there's an old real estate saying that goes "buyers are liars." Lots of well-meaning agents believe that buyers are "time wasters" and not worth their effort. My confession is that I used to think that way, too. I'm embarrassed to admit that early in my career I went through a period where I felt that the financial return on working with buyers was too often not worth the time investment.

But now? Buyers? Liars?

Wrong. *Not. Even. Close.*

It's way past the time to retire that silly phrase because I am 100% certain that *most* buyers are *not* liars. In fact, I'm going to take it miles further:

If you don't love working with buyers it's because you don't know how to work with them.

Because buyers are *not* liars and *if coached correctly* — from first contact through close of escrow — buyers are *anything* but time wasters. Buyers are in fact the very best way to make money *fast* in real estate.

To repeat: buyers are the very best way to make money *fast* in real estate.

> **If you don't love working with buyers it's because you don't know how to work with them.**

9

The first, most common misperception about buyers is that if you work with them it will take, at best, three or four weeks to get paid and, in a worst-case scenario, many months or even years to finally see your commission.

That *is* too long. So I'm going to help you fix that by teaching you how to coach buyers so that they work for *you!*

In short, you could meet a buyer tomorrow, show him property, and get paid in 10 days (superfast closes coming up in Chapter 4). A $300,000 sale? That's a $9,000 commission (at 3%) you could have in just 10 days.

As my father is fond of saying, "Not too shabby!"

Now, *I think* I know what you are thinking: being a listing agent is an *unlimited* avenue to making money.

Agreed.

You can have 100 listings but you can't have 100 buyers.

I understand. Believe me, *I love listings.* Listings are the surest way to achieve long-term success and durability in real estate.

But if you have immediate financial needs (or if you're the type of agent that refuses to let a golden opportunity slip by), then buyers are the best way to address those needs.

What's more, if you are willing to adopt *and embrace* what I'm about to tell you, then you can become an expert at working with buyers, which is virtually a license to print money fast!

In this chapter I'm going to teach you how to work with buyers so they don't work you over. I'm going to teach you how to control the relationship with buyers so that you maximize your time and energy, and come out with a fast sale and a repeat client. Because even if you don't have immediate financial needs, mastering how to maximize working with buyers is an integral part of real estate success and should absolutely *never* be taken for granted or overlooked. Simply, don't waste opportunity. *Utilize* coachable buyers to make quick, easy, *consistent* money that supplements your work with sellers.

I'm big on setting the proper foundation for success, so what I want you to do is to begin to think differently about buyers.

But first, back to confession time: I have to restate this because I want you to understand how I was once a wrong-headed thinker. Like many people in real estate, I once saw buyers as a necessary evil (at best). I didn't like the process, the pace, the trouble, and oftentimes I didn't like the end result of working with buyers.

> **Think differently about buyers.**

Show them houses for weeks and weeks, and end up right back at the start, working with someone who refuses to make an offer on a house.

But my having been there, my having disliked working with buyers, is *exactly* why I can help you get over those feelings. Because along the way I've gotten to the point where I've become *so comfortable and so versed* in the art of working with buyers that, on a challenge, I was able to set the *realistic goal* of getting 30 buyers to buy in 30 days. NOT 30 buyers in one year: *30 buyers in 30 days.*

You simply have to control the buyer relationship from start to finish.

I usually sell a buyer a home the first or, at most, the second time I'm out with them. I can do this because I dictate the entire process right from the get-go. The phone rings, it's a buyer, and I am in charge of the transaction.

> **You simply have to control the buyer relationship from start to finish.**

You Are Completely in Control of the Process

It's a nightmare. You've shown a buyer 10, 15, or even 20 different houses all over town, you've spent your time, money and energy on them, and they didn't buy. You may be wondering: How can I be in control of that?

Let's start with ways to maximize your odds of putting buyers into homes. First, from the moment the phone rings and you have your initial conversation with a buyer, you need to set unbreakable boundaries and rules. You must set the tone and the guidelines that they *must* follow.

You don't do this to be a hard person or to be arrogant. Not at all. But what this *does mean* is that you are actually going to pass on working with uncoachable buyers.

> **You need to set unbreakable boundaries and rules.**

That's right. Good market? Bad market? It doesn't matter. At the same time you are moving clients toward buying a house, right from the *very first conversation* you are going to maintain your criteria for weeding out uncoachable buyers.

There'll be no exceptions.

And even if this means jettisoning 20%, or more, of the buyers who come your way, you are going to weed them out and pass them along. And yet, *because* you are weeding them out, you are going to be busier and make more money *faster* than ever before.

Even in a recession.

Who Is "Coachable" and Who Isn't?

Most buyers are coachable. You're going to learn that. But life isn't 100% perfect and some people are just not going to allow you to lead. So, how do you quickly tell who is "coachable" and who isn't?

First aside: Difficult buyer? Maybe even a jerk? It's not a total loss, because if you have an uncoachable buyer who refuses to let you dictate the process that I'm about to outline here, then you *immediately* refer him out for a 25% fee and move on (or, if they are a sociopath, you jettison them completely). There are absolutely no second or third chances because that's poor time management and "poor time management" is not what I'm teaching.

Again, having rules that you *insist* your buyers *and you yourself* follow is not to be hardheaded or prideful. This is so that you will maximize your time and your energy over a *long period* of time — because both in the present, and also over the extended body of your career, *not wasting your time and energy makes you a lot more money.*

And that means jettisoning uncoachable buyers 100% of the time.

You need to draw the following lines in the sand because we are in a business like any other. If you own a car dealership, you don't give your cars away for free. You'd be out of business in a week. Well, in real estate, the only thing you yourself own is your time. And to be successful you've got to *jealously* guard that time.

Simple math can illustrate to you your time and energy output versus your return, and prove to you where you need to put your energy and focus. It can also show you how much time and energy you should expend on someone before you move on and put those valuable personal commodities into someone else.

You've no doubt heard the saying "Don't throw good money after bad." Well, as with money, you shouldn't throw good time after bad. You must never allow yourself to think, "I've already spent two days on these people, so I might as well keep going." No sir. You'll only work with people who will follow your guidelines and allow you to do your job. And this is where you learn to weed out the uncoachable buyers (and we'll get to "lead generation" soon enough) and move on, because as you'll soon see, moving on will actually make you more money in the long run.

> You'll only work with people who will follow your guidelines and allow you to do your job.

Take a Buyer Out a Maximum of Three Times

I take buyers out a maximum of three times. That's right! I take buyers out three times *at most!*

Now, after reading that, if you are one of the many realtors saying to yourself, "I take my buyers out 10 or even 15 times, often for a year or two!" Then what I say to you is that you are wasting your time and very much limiting your potential for income.

And if you are indeed an agent who has recently taken a buyer out 5, 10, or even 15 times, then it's no wonder buyers have such a bad reputation in our business: it's our fault for not training them. If you take a buyer out 10 times you have wasted as much as 60 or 70 hours (or more) of your time.

There's not much mystery here because this is about a statistical return on your time investment. Three times out with a buyer may seem arbitrary, but it's not, and you'll soon see why. You *must* stick to this rule! If you take a buyer out three times and they haven't made an offer, then you immediately farm them out to an associate (and take your 25% referral fee as soon as they do buy).

Now, the lone exception, the gray area here, would be if you took a buyer out three times and on the third trip out they wrote an offer that just flat got beat. That's a buyer you can live with for another day (though I'm going to teach you how to structure offers that almost never get beat, as well). Or if the buyer wants to make an offer and you find that the home just went "pending." These types of buyers qualify for another outing, but only because they have proven they are willing to pull the trigger.

> **If you take a buyer out three times and they haven't made an offer, then you immediately farm them out to an associate.**

Buyers who are willing to buy are the ones we want.

Three trips out, no offer, so then you farm them out? You *might* be thinking that I'm being harsh. Or maybe you're wondering whether I care about my buyer's needs. The answer is . . . Yes! I care. My repeat clients and complex referral trees show I care and, *most importantly*, they show that my clients know that I care. However, I *also* care about my family's needs, as well.

Early in my career I spent thousands of hours driving around with perfectly nice window-shoppers who I would later learn had no intention of buying a house that year. Your family does not need you out spinning your wheels and spending *your* money in the name of over-the-top customer attentiveness. Your family, and you, the businessperson, need to learn to quickly differentiate between looky-loos and serious buyers.

Farm Them Out and Move On

I'm the last person you would describe as a math whiz. But I do know that in business, over time, statistics bear out certain absolute truths based on a consistent performance and effort and return on your investment (time). You *need* to be consistent to be successful, and maintaining that regularity is how you want to run your business each and every single day. You maximize results by being consistent. The result, *in the end* — if you are 100% consistent with the quick elimination of uncoachable buyers — will be more net sales and more money for you, because, first, you'll sell the coachable buyers fast. Second, you'll jettison uncoachable buyers, wasting a minimum of time and freeing you up to work with coachable buyers (more on that later). Third, you'll develop a strong revenue stream of referrals.

Years of working with buyers has proved to me that three times out with no offers means trouble. It's important to note that this doesn't mean that, say, one or two people you cut loose might not just need one more showing to find their house. Sure. *Occasionally*, the agent you've farmed someone out to will say, "Hey, thanks for the referral. They bought the first house we looked at."

But that's the exception and not the rule. And that's just fine! Don't try and predict the exceptions. Remember: this isn't only about three times out. You are going to coach these buyers to drastically up the odds of them making an offer. So it's not about three trips out with any old buyer. It's about three specialized trips out with well-trained buyers. It's about using a method that I'm going to outline that ensures offers. This allows you to draw these very precise lines in the sand. Three times out and no offer? You farm them out 100% of the time.

I'm Scared to Lose Clients

Times are tough. Clients are hard to come by. How can I let one go?

I get this line of thinking.

One of the reasons agents won't let go of buyers is because they have a limited number of clients. But that's faulty thinking. First, efficient lead generation will increase your number of clients. (Lead generation techniques coming up in Chapter 2.) Second, if in a single year you have even 10 problem buyers who you take out, say, even three extra times per buyer, that's 30 *extra* shopping sessions at an average of five hours per session, or 150 hours of your time wasted, minimum! (Not to mention money, wear and tear, and your valuable energy.) Whether you calculate your time as being worth $50, $100, or $1,000 per hour, you don't have 150 hours to waste window shopping!

Using those 150 hours to build your business by training, by utilizing lead generation techniques, by refining your business; those 150 hours are three weeks of your work and time. Time you can use to build your business and implement the lessons I have here.

Don't live in fear. The trade-off is worth it.

Besides, if a buyer who you've just farmed out buys right after the referral, *that's absolutely great!* How could that be bad? Everyone wins. A healthy number of referral fees is an important part of your plan. To repeat: referral fees are a part of your business. You are creating revenue streams. And, in spite of the occasional quick buyer who you've passed along, more often than not — after three showings in which you've had plenty of opportunity to measure the intention of the buyer — three outings can just as quickly

> A healthy number of referral fees is an important part of your plan.

become 10 or even 15 outings. Your hourly wage is falling with each passing minute! Your expenditures are rising and your opportunity to earn money is dropping.

It's nothing personal, so don't take it personally (even if you like the buyer). Pass slow or difficult buyers along! They may be the greatest people on earth, but three times up to bat with no swings and you send them off to another agent.

Here's what I do: I set the fourth appointment up and then I refer them to the best buyer's agent I can find. Let them know you are passing them along to a pro (as long as you mean it). Then let the agent know what you've learned. Let the agent know everything you know about the buyers. Where you've looked and what they've said and what they've done. You want him to succeed. Maximize *his* knowledge about the buyers. Make it as easy for him as possible. Pass them on and then move on. And remember, the better the agent that you refer them to, the better the odds that you'll receive your 25% referral!

Time Out with Buyers

I allot two hours to show properties to any single client on any one trip out. Two. I know agents who spend the entire day with a client, driving from property to property. That may sound noble, but it's a mistake for you *and* for your client. Because if you can spend an entire day with one client, then you don't have enough buyers. It's that simple (unless you are a boutique agent whose business revolves around selling just 12–18 homes per year). And if you spend an entire day with a client, because buying a house is emotional and your client is relying on you to show them what they are looking for, you are setting your client (and yourself) up for indecisiveness because you are not creating a sense of urgency. You need to provide the peaks and valleys of the shopping experience.

> I allot two hours to show properties to any single client on any one trip out.

What about a scenario where there are actually 14 really good properties to show the client? Then you need to show them five to seven one weekend, and five to seven the next (much, *much more* on the importance of "showing order," a prime component of your successful "working with buyers" business model, coming up!).

It's very important that you don't tell your buyer, "I have 14 great houses to show you!" Right now, you have five to seven. That's all. You have two hours. That's all. If you tell them about the homes you'll show them next weekend, then they'll want to go right then, or, worse, they'll look at each house as part of a whole and not as a product to be either purchased or passed over. Besides, buyers (and you, also) are shopped out after 5–7 properties. If you keep going and show them 15–20 houses, everything begins to look the same! Confusion sets in!

I wish we could all work with one client each month, showing them Beverly Hills mansions and then stopping off for brunch at the Ritz Carlton. The moment the buyer makes a decision on a $7 million property — always in less than 30 days — the next client is waiting at the Chateau Marmont on Sunset Boulevard, and she insists that she will only work with *you*.

Surprise! That's not how it works for 99.9% of the agents out there. You are learning to maximize your time and increase your sales. And this is how you do it. You are not being rude by spending a maximum of two hours with a client. You are not being unprofessional. You are the professional! You are in control of the session and the transaction! And five to seven *strategically presented* houses in a day is plenty, because I promise you this: if you show someone more than seven houses in a day, they are not only NOT going to trust you or trust what they've seen, they will need to go back again and again and again to each plausible property to compare each closet and each garage, and

> **You are the professional! You are in control of the session and the transaction!**

this shower and that yard. You show them five to seven maximum, and then you go and meet with another client.

Once more, Chapter 2, "Dynamic Powerful Open Houses" is a sister chapter to "Buyers Are the Gift of Gold," and I am going to teach you everything you need to know to accumulate 10, 20, or even 30 clients in a single weekend, so we won't cover that now (even though I want to). Needless to say, by utilizing the coming lessons outlined in *Momentum,* you are going to accumulate enough clients so that you can't hold open houses on Saturdays anymore because you have so many serious buyers to work with and show properties to. The goal is to *quickly* get to the point where you can't even hold open houses *every* Sunday anymore (Saturdays, of course, are long since filled up). You are showing homes to 4–5 buyers every Saturday and showing homes to 4–5 buyers every Sunday. That's 8–10 buyers a weekend! (And exactly what I call "Momentum in real estate!")

The Important Psychology of Showing Order

Showing order is one of those things that seems small but is actually HUGE. In fact, I love the psychology of showing order.

First, some reminders on the actual presentation of homes: Have discipline! Don't try to "sell" your buyer every single house they see. Because this is not just a race, it's a *strategic* race. In fact, this may surprise you, but as a way to

> **Show your client some houses that they would never purchase.**

get your buyer to appreciate the house you actually *expect* them to buy, you are first going to show your client some houses that they would never purchase.

Many realtors think they've got to put their sales hat on and sell every house to each client as though their life depended on it. Here's a tip: it doesn't. "What if *they* love it?" you're thinking. When you get excited about a house that your client has no business buying you are only wasting your time and threatening your credibility.

Be secure that you are the professional. Be patient that this is a process and that you have a goal in mind. As you will soon see, showing order is an art. It is *that* specific. And because showing order increases sales, and actually *decreases* the amount of time you'll need to spend with each buyer — it's just one of the changes that make working with buyers more profitable and more efficient than you previously imagined.

> **Showing order is an art.**

Earlier, I said you will pick the best five to seven houses to show your buyer. A little preview: we are *not* showing our buyers seven houses and hoping to sell him one of the seven. We are showing our buyer seven houses and *expecting* to sell him the sixth or the seventh house (or, in cases where we have five houses to show our client, the fifth).

The first few houses I show a client I do so with the plan that I'm *purposely* showing them the *worst choices first* to get them ready for the house they will actually buy. You march in, look around, check the client, and then call a dog a dog and move on to the next house. Don't be the least bit fearful of pointing out a negative property. In fact, *do it!* They'll appreciate you for it and they'll trust you more. Save the positive enthusiasm for the house they are likely to buy. You want to show the worst homes first and the best homes last. This may not sound like much, but there's a reason it's effective, which I'll explain in a minute.

With a typical buyer, the second house is important. As for the first house, I show them something I know they'll never buy. I'm not saying you show them a shack, but show them something you *know* is the least desirable property on the schedule, and then you join with them in a full-fledged retreat out of there! Show the seven best homes you can find, but show your buyer the worst of the seven first!

Be brave, and have faith in yourself to allow this to work.

The second house I show my buyer is just okay. Noticeably better than house #1, but still not a house you'd encourage them to ever buy. It's bigger, cleaner, and in better shape than house #1. But that's about it.

Then I escalate. Each house I show them is better than the last, until we get to number five, six, or seven (seven is the maximum number of houses, depending on how many I have to show), with the last one being the best house of all.

I'll say it again: Showing order is crucial to selling on the first trip out. Start low and then build momentum. Experience and trial and error have proved to me that the showing order is absolutely essential to working with buyers and getting them prepared to buy the very first day.

> **Showing order is crucial to selling on the first trip out.**

It's like surfing. I was born in San Diego. I've surfed a bit. And sure, surfers like to sit out on their boards and soak in the sun. They like bantering back and forth with their mates, just hoping for some decent waves. But what gets *real* surfers the most excited is right when they are hitting the curl of the wave.

Ever listen to a surfer talk about surfing? That curl of the wave is what they live for.

It's the same with buyers. You get them to the sixth home, it's the best so far, and they are ready to jump out of their skin. Each house has been an improvement over the previous house, and they are getting excited. Their juices are flowing. They feel positive. It's #6 and they want to buy right then, but you have something better up your sleeve. You aren't *nearly* through yet!

Here comes the curl of the wave.

This is *your* plan. And *your* plan differs from most other agents' plans. Most other agents base their showing order on geography — driving the shortest distance from house to house to house. Driving the shortest distance to show houses is a huge mistake! Geography, as it pertains to showing order, is an afterthought!

In my showing order, do I ever cover the same ground twice?

Absolutely! (Though not nearly as often as you might think.) But I don't care where the homes are located, and by the end of our appointment, the buyer won't, either. This is about preparing the buyer to buy. It's about the appetite of human nature, which is tempted by *escalation*. Besides, I'm the agent and the buyer doesn't know my route. And even if they are ultrafamiliar with the area, it doesn't matter because this is a roller coaster and I'm in charge. They don't care about route! I'm showing them the starter house, then an okay house (which they are *very* relieved to see after the starter), and then we start the climb up the track to the peak of the ride. Click. Click. Click. You know how the older roller coasters climb and the wheels click as they move you upward toward the crest? Click. Click. Click. Well, each house on *my* tour is another rung up the ramp of the roller coaster. We're surfing, baby! The excitement is building as we go up and up and up and up, AND HERE COMES THE CURL!

> Geography, as it pertains to showing order, is an afterthought!

And then the crest! The sunset! They reach the peak! The perfect house! And they are jumping out of their skin to make an offer!

Buying is a mindset. When you take someone to a house that they would never under any circumstances buy, their emotions sink and they think, "We'll never find a good-enough house." But then you take them to a house that they would still probably never buy, but which is better than house #1, and that shift in perception and hopefulness charges their brain with possibility and optimism. Then #3 is okay, but still not what they were *hoping* for, but gosh darn! Now we're talking! Then #4 actually has some nice qualities — they're breathing easier and are actually trying to talk themselves into buying. *Emotionally*, something happens to the "buyer" *inside* people as their expectations rise and they get excited. Disappointment turns to hope. Their adrenaline is starting to pump. Their mood is lighter and they are *extremely* curious about house #5, which is — you point out — located right smack dab in the middle of the best school district in town. And *not only* that, but the bathrooms are new! #5 is a house they might actually buy, especially after the first four. It's also the first house that you are actually pre-selling to them in order to get them excited.

And now they *are* excited.

But you've got something better in store for them. Something better? YES! Because house #5 was nice, but it's not *nearly* as good as house #6. Just wait until they see house #6, because #6 is a very nice house!

For the first time *even you* are enthusiastic. *Now* you are beginning to sell the assets of the house. #6 is not perfect — though it could be, and you may even point out how — but #6 is "almost" great and both you *and* the buyer like *just about* everything about house #6.

(If you are doing your job, the buyer may even tell you they want to make an offer on #6. Remember, any seven houses can be placed in order from worst to first, and this will get your buyer ready to buy when #6 comes along.)

But then you tell them, "That (#6) was a good house, but I've been saving the best for last."

And it's over. The climbing, the ascending, the waiting for the perfect wave, they want to buy and, emotionally, they simply can't wait for what comes next. They want to buy a house and their emotions and moods have been lifted by the fact that each home is measurably better than the last.

It's just how we human beings are built. And once you whet our appetites, we are hungry for the next course. Why do you think restaurants bring a dessert tray to the table? We just ate! Aren't we full? No. We are chomping at the bit for what comes next. So I always save the best for last, no matter where it lays on my route. It could be just down the street from the first house, but that doesn't matter.

Ideally, my last house is owned by a motivated seller who needs to sell fast. They've just put $100,000 into the kitchen and painted it because they just *could not* live in a house that was not in prime condition in every way. I cover research quite a bit later on, so understand that you need to know the houses on your showing order, and I'll teach you how.

First, a little bit about green living and the route. A common mistake that most buyer agents make is that they MapQuest the route and conduct their appointments by geography. They want to save on gas and time and go green, which seems perfectly noble. And it works great! (When you are shopping for shoes, that is.)

But it doesn't work in real estate. It's neither cost-effective nor is it time-effective to MapQuest your route in the hope of saving time, going green, or making money. In fact, in this instance, attempting to go green is an energy-wasting mistake that will actually burn more fuel and turn out to do everything but save money and resources.

The longer "escalating route" of showing order will have your buyer *buying faster*, and will save on gas, time, and wear and tear on you, your clients, and your car.

Is showing order just a little thing in the big scheme of your business?

Did you ever complete something that didn't turn out quite the way you had planned, and then you asked yourself, "What could I have done differently?" Ever consider what the margin is between victory and defeat? I don't believe there are "little things" in business. But let me again say this: you want to maximize your time so that you make more money. You want to streamline your schedule and get *more* out of the time you already put into your business.

So, is showing order a little thing? Not in my book. If you master showing order, and if you develop the confidence to lead, you will be taking a GIANT step forward on the path to increasing your income and streamlining your business. I know agents who spend a year with a certain buyer and then believe that because they have invested so much time they simply *must* ride it out. They have to stay until the finish.

Those agents will be finished, all right. Because those habits are not loyal or smart. That's throwing good money (and precious time) after bad.

Uncoachable buyer? Three times out with five to seven homes shown in escalating order, and still no offers? Cut your losses and move on, now!

Worst to first. I may go to the far side of town for the first house. Zip back toward the office to show the second. Then it's on to another part of town to show the third. Then it's back to the south side for #4. Here I am zigzagging back and forth across town. Am I wasting time or money? No way! I'm *building momentum*. At first glance it may not *appear* to be the greenest way to show, but in the end it literally saves barrels of oil because you usually need to do this only once. You sell the buyer a house in a single day instead of weeks or even months. It's actually *much, much greener* when you work smart.

> Three times out with five to seven homes shown in escalating order, and still no offers? Cut your losses and move on, now!

When you show a buyer a great house in the first two or three stops — and they fall in love with it — and then you show them something average that's on your green route, it stops your momentum and it clouds their minds. The great house they saw isn't nearly so great when they see crummy or average houses right after. They may still love the great house, but now they are uncertain and they are going to want to see more houses because of this uncertainty. It's human nature. Buyers buy because they are excited, motivated, and worried that the opportunity will pass them by. They buy because, emotionally, they are prepared to buy and their emotions are being satisfied by desirable homes shown in ascending order. Buyers buy because they've had a natural upswing of choices and *that* makes the choice obvious and easy *and* urgent.

Does the buyer realize the route is roundabout? Almost never. First, sometimes it isn't *actually* roundabout at all. Maybe it's a circle. Maybe it's a star. The above example of north, south, east and then west showings is pretty rare. Second, their minds are elsewhere and they are entrusting me to help them find a house, not act as a chauffeur. You're not trying to *fool* them into buying or taking a joy ride. Sales is an art. It's drama. It's emotional. It's salsa dancing!

If you are worried about it, just remind them, "I've saved these for last because I wanted you to know what was out there."

Believe me, no one is getting mad.

You ever notice how when *you* are a passenger in a car, even if you are going someplace you've been a thousand times, the trip is *completely* different from when you are in the driver's seat? By the time the day is over, your buyer is going to have a house, so the route matters less than just about anything. Finding my buyer a house is what I am going to do. They need to trust me, and if they question me, they won't be questioning me for long.

Legendary UCLA basketball coach and author John Wooden passed away in 2010 at 99 years of age. Wooden was a beloved figure whose impact was felt far beyond basketball. He was a poet and a philosopher. He wrote dozens of books and is a hero to presidents and CEOs alike. One of the things he was known to have said to his players was, "Be quick, but don't hurry."

That's what I do. It's not because I'm special or a nice guy that my buyers make offers and buy houses. I've learned that the sequence of showings matters as much as the house itself. Again, the sequence matters as much as the house itself! It's just how we're made and I've learned to work with that. My buyer's excitement when I show them the fifth or seventh property motivates them to make an offer — which in turn gets them the house. Because one of my biggest strengths as an agent is that I manage expectations. And because I manage expectations in ways large and small, my clients end up with their dream homes.

Questions You *Must* Ask *Before* You Go

The way I figure out what it is that my buyers want in a house is to simply ask a series of questions. And I do not take on, or take out, a buyer until they have satisfactorily answered them.

- What cities or suburbs would you like to live in?
- What is your price range?
- How many bedrooms and baths do you require?
- What's the minimum square footage you will consider?
- What's the minimum lot size you will consider?
- Two- or three-car garage?
- Are two stories okay?
- Would you like a pool?
- What else is important to you? (Do you want a view, privacy, school district, or a gourmet kitchen?).

I absolutely *must* know the answers to *every one* of these questions *before* I take a buyer out on an appointment. By getting solid answers, I save valuable time and money and can deliver my clients to what they want — which brings me what I want.

But you'll never know until you ask. And here's a warning as important as any in *Momentum*: if you wait until you are out with your buyer showing houses to kick ideas around and learn these things, you are wasting a colossal amount of time and energy. Not just yours, but theirs, too. And because shopping for a home can be stressful, and because buyers *justifiably* want you to know your business (i.e., read their minds) they will get irritated with you if you have set aside an entire morning to show them five two-story houses when the one thing they *don't* want is a two-story house.

Don't expect them to tell you unless you ask. Usually you are dealing with couples and they have more than one mind and what's *vitally* important to one, and somewhat important to the other, becomes *vitally* important when it comes to buying a home. Many times early in my career I stood inside a house where the husband said, "This is great!" Only to have the wife say, "We can't have a two-story house with a baby." You need to ask these questions up-front. *Right during the first telephone call.* Then, later, you ask clarifying questions. Your clients will love your interest in getting to the heart of their wants. Asking the right questions will put them at ease and let them know that not only are you in charge, but *you* are the right man or woman for the job.

Be quick, but don't hurry. Be thorough, and then be even *more* thorough.

Now, certain answers are not etched in stone. Some people are flexible on countertops and even the number of rooms; things that might be *extremely* important to you or me. Doesn't matter. If you ask these questions *every time*, you will reduce your margin of error and speed up the rate of purchase *considerably*.

Buyer Motivation: Closing Buyers with Cold Feet

As an agent working with a buyer, *occasionally* it won't matter what you do. You can be the greatest agent on earth, and it can be the greatest house and the best deal in the history of civilization, but sometimes, none of that matters. Sometimes, buyers just get cold feet. It happens to the best of us. It's human nature.

But just because a buyer is getting cold feet doesn't mean you have to lose your sale. It's time for you to go to work. There's a strategy to follow here. First, however, you have to identify what's going on.

One of the most common ways buyers stall happens like this: you show a house and it's *absolutely perfect*. The buyers can't believe it. They walk around, mouths wide as train tunnels, and everything is perfect and you know — *you just know* — that it's a done deal.

But then you notice the couple discussing it just between themselves a little bit. Maybe they are whispering. Maybe there's irritation in their body language. Suddenly, their demeanor changes and they want to go to dinner and talk about it.

It's a huge decision and they probably *should* discuss it.

But at dinner — *away* from the perfect house — things just get worse and they start to cool off.

The time for them to call comes — and they do — but now they want to sleep on it.

You are about to lose your sale. By the next morning it will be "What house?"

Momentum is written for people in our industry. I never take the weight of the decisions of my buyers lightly, but I'm not writing these words for buyers. I'm talking to you, agents and brokers. From a young couple that is just starting out, all the way to mature folks who have purchased half a dozen homes in their lifetimes, to a bachelor with a new corporate gig and money to burn, $175,000, $300,000, $400,000, $500,000, $1 million. These are HUGE, *binding* transactions and some serious introspection and caution are in order.

But because I am speaking to you, I am speaking with the goal of making deals happen. *Not* at someone's expense, mind you. *But these people are going to buy a house from someone!* This is a business and the better you are at your business the more sales you will close. As long as you know your job and are a pro, you might as well help them buy from you.

Over the course of your career, the more houses you show the more different types of personalities and scenarios you will encounter. Never do harm. Never push someone who truly doesn't feel ready to buy. But at the same time remember: they are in the market and they are going to buy from someone.

So what should you do?

You can help them see the forest *and the trees* and appreciate the house that — because you've asked the right questions — is the right house for them.

So, when a buyer sees a house that you know is a great deal — it meets all their criteria — and when they express to you that they love the property, that it's the best they've seen and that they really, *really* want it ... but they ... just ... have ... to ... think ... about it ... over ... dinner (or, worse, if they want to wait until the next morning), for no other reason than cold feet, you are about to lose a sale that they *should* make, and worse, you are about to enter into a business relationship that, if allowed, will drag out over months and months.

And *that* is bad for you.

Want to avoid losing sales that you *absolutely should make?* Here's how: if the buyer loves the house, but wants to wait until the morning, I pull them aside and I tell them that they should write the offer right then. I explain to them that if they wait until morning they *very much run the risk* of being in a multiple offer situation.

Multiple offers mean no control.

But if they write an offer right then, they have the opportunity to get that offer accepted *that night*, which puts them in the decision-maker's seat.

This is business. If they feel they have control, and they *know* they've got an ally in you, their agent, then *you* have control.

And when they ask, "What if I change my mind?" *That's* what "control" really means.

I tell buyers that it's better to have their offer accepted and later change their minds than to want the property and not be able to get it. I may even tell them how many times I've seen it happen. *They* don't want to lose the chance to buy this house. And that's just *one thing* they risk if they wait.

What else do they risk by waiting? They may realize what you, and probably they, *already* know: that it's the perfect house and they want it! Then, because they waited, they get stuck in a bidding war over a property they could have had the night before just by having written an offer. Either way, if they want the property, then I tell them it's in their best interest to make that offer. And I explain this so they *completely* understand that it's in *their best interest* anyway you slice it.

Waiting = Multiple Offers = Bidding Wars = No Control

The worst thing a buyer can do is wait — it only invites competition and muddies the waters. No one wants to be in a bidding war. And besides, INCREDIBLY, the best time to make an offer is when they aren't 1,000% sure that they want the property. Because once they decide they *have* to have the property — and a bidding war breaks out — then they *will absolutely pay more!* But if they aren't totally sure, then they can comfortably offer *less.* That's when you make a $375,000 offer on a house that is *actually* worth $400,000.

> I tell buyers that it's better to have their offer accepted and later change their minds than to want the property and not be able to get it.

This matters. This is good business for you and for your buyer. *And this works.*

You miss 100% of the shots you don't take. If the buyer can get a house for $25,000 less than it's actually worth *just because she's made the first offer*, then that simply sweetens the deal.

Everything Is Perfect and Yet They Still Won't Buy

People mask fear in procrastination. What do you do if you're afraid to jump out of a perfectly good airplane? You hesitate. You procrastinate. You say things like, "I need a minute." "I need some time to think about it." But the more you think about it, the more hesitant you get about the decision you need to make.

Have you ever jumped off a *really* high diving board? Have you every bungee-jumped or parachuted? You're up there ready to go — you've already paid your money — and yet you just can't quite pull the trigger and go.

So here's a question as it relates to making the jump: does it get easier the longer you wait?

I've seen people who *absolutely loved* a particular house break into a cold sweat and be completely unable to speak because of the fear associated with the size of the purchase. Encouraging people to embrace that fear by allowing them to wait only means they will miss the opportunity at hand. *This* is one of the things that you're there to help them avoid. Otherwise, even robots could show buyers houses and then simply step aside and wait for them to freeze up.

Simply, part of *your* job is to convince them to jump. It's now *your* job to sell them the house, and to convince them that it's what they wanted *based* on how they answered your questions and what you know about the market. You have them at the door of the airplane, and now it's time to give them a little help. *How* you nudge them, your style, it will vary some from buyer to buyer. But make no mistake, if you do your job and get them in a position to buy the house of their dreams, *sometimes* you have to give them a little . . . push.

What about the buyer who finds the perfect house, but even balks at making a Hail Mary offer that is $25,000 below asking? If you are now dealing with a buyer who was excited as all get-out for the house when it was $400,000, but then got cold feet — say they are just about ready to make the $375,000 offer, but are still hesitating — then what I do is tell them to take a shot. I tell them to offer $345,000 and see what happens.

You must remember what your ultimate goal is: you're trying to make a sale. And sales begin with offers. And this method of just getting them to make an offer — *any offer* — gets the ball rolling so that the game can begin. But it does something else, as well. Getting them to make even, I have to admit, a ridiculous offer, this gets the process of buying started and keeps the transaction from carrying on for months and months.

If you get them to make an offer, any offer, the next offer will come much more easily.

Your time is valuable. And just like any other job — with a little simple division — at the end of the year you can figure out *exactly* how much money you made per hour. Those hours you spent letting buyers walk away from great properties because of fear? Those *additional* hours (or days or weeks or months) that you now must spend holding that buyer's hand? Those wasted hours do not make you a better person. They do not make you friends for life with that buyer. Those wasted hours make you a poorer businessperson.

> If you get them to make an offer, any offer, the next offer will come much more easily.

Don't forget that.

Again: there are two important things happening with an *initial* low-ball offer: FIRST, a low-ball offer may well get Mr. Buyer a great house. And SECOND, it gets Mr. Buyer moving and ready to make a deal. If you can't convince the buyer to swing the bat, then nobody has a chance for success.

Remember, making offers is 100% risk-free. If in 10 or 14 days the buyer decides to cancel the sale, then the sale can be canceled. The fail-safe here is the 17-day contingency law (each state varies some, so make sure you know *your* state's contingency law). I tell Mr. Buyer that the reality is that they aren't going to make the actual decision to buy the house for 17 days. This not only gives them *real time* to reflect and make up their minds, it *also* gives them control. If they are actually dragging their feet on even making a simple offer on, say, the single greatest house in the history of the universe, they are going to be waiting and hesitating a long, *long* time. That $1,000 an hour you hope to make in your business? When you work with people like this and let them control the transaction with procrastination, then your income is going to drop because you are going to spend dozens of extra hours with these probably very fine — but in-decisive — people, waiting for them to make up their minds.

The simple truth here is that everyone is looking for a leader. Lead! No matter what your personality, the laid-back, "I'm my buyer's best friend" style of real estate PALES in comparison to actually knowing what you are doing. "Competence" is king. Being the great guy or gal is actually lazy and not all that cool. *Know* your market. *Know* what your buyer wants. Help them find what they are looking for and then get them to make an offer.

But, to back up a little bit, working with hesitant buyers is actually the worst-case scenario you'll face. Remember, you are going to accumulate more buyers than you ever thought imaginable! And you are *actually* going to farm some of these buyers out to other realtors for your 25% referral fee. Your business model is to have so many buyers that you only have time to work with *decisive* clients. The *coachable* ones. Once you streamline your practice and learn how to quickly put buyers in the deciding mode, you control your business and are maximizing your time and energy. And *that* is when real estate becomes a delight! That is when you have your business cranking!

What you *have* to explain to the buyer is that they are not buying the house just because they are making an offer. They are setting themselves up to decide whether or not they want the house. They are taking control, possibly avoiding multiple offers and price wars, and giving themselves the option to buy *and* the time to make up their minds.

Again, you are selling *control*. You are selling *choice*. You are moving the business relationship into a stadium that is home field for you. You are creating momentum for the eventual purchase.

Take another moment and put yourself in their shoes. While buying a house is a huge deal, making an offer actually takes the pressure off. *Especially* when they aren't 100% certain.

I have a lot of friends who have worked in retail. And the #1 question that customers ask retail salespeople is: what's your return policy? *Real estate has a return policy.* USE IT TO YOUR

ADVANTAGE! (In fact, use those exact words: return policy.) Big purchase or small purchase, a return policy allows people to make up their minds. In the beginning, the goal is to get the seller to agree to price and terms. If that can be accomplished, then the next step is for the buyer to decide over the next 17 days whether they *actually* want the house or not. It's a great deal. It's a test drive. And it's a great opportunity for you to get the

> **Real estate has a return policy.**

buyer in the driver's seat and get them comfortable with overcoming a huge obstacle to buying: pulling the trigger.

Most of us have been with buyers who *dearly* loved a house but were afraid to commit. Well, the 17-day inspection/due diligence period gives them both a gentle, safe in and a gentle, safe out and allows them to proceed at a comfortable pace. It puts the buyer at ease. It makes the buyer feel calm. It's good for everyone and is the best way to take the fear out of the transaction. But, all too often, agents just ask their buyer if they want to make an offer on the house. What the buyer is thinking is, "Do I really want to spend $290,000 right now?" Then they worry themselves sleepless thinking it's all a big irreversible mistake.

This is when YOU emphatically state, with additional chutzpah *as needed*, that they (your buyers) are not buying the house right then, they are just tying it up, getting it off the market, exclusively reserving it for themselves! This way, THEY can spend the next couple of *weeks* deciding whether they want to purchase this exact house.

The best part of this great real estate moment? You are about to get paid because the really, really terrific thing is, *the very second* they finish writing the offer, they go home and then they can't help but call their family and friends and announce that they've bought a house. In the next few days they will drive by that house 100 times — they *literally* stalk that house because it's theirs! Because they own it! They are now emotionally attached, and any warts that house has can be smoothed over with a little love — love that the new owners, YOUR BUYERS, have now developed for their house.

Sign Calls and Internet Leads: Making Them Time-, Resource-, and Energy-Efficient

Guess what? I LOVE SIGN CALLS! And I usually run right out and do them. But first, I ask the caller, "Do you like houses in that *exact* area?"

I then tell them that I know of some great deals out there, which I follow up by asking, "Is this the price range you are shopping in?" Then it's on to me asking them to tell me *exactly* what they are looking for — and once they tell me that, I entice them further by telling them that I will bring a couple of homes with me that will blow their minds!

I do this because, while buyers *rarely* purchase the house they call about, "sign calls" are an opportunity to meet a motivated buyer.

Many agents drive on over and show only the *one house* the buyer called about. Big mistake! If you take a moment to ask the buyer some defining questions, you can bring along some matching properties and capitalize on the opportunity. Then it becomes like eHarmony for home shoppers.

Okay, we are building and increasing business, so let's *make* sign calls worth your time. Here's what I do to not *only* enhance my chances of making a sale, but to make sign calls pay in one way or another almost every time.

Before heading out the door to meet the buyer from the sign call, jump on the computer and get yourself two emergency backup, cleanup hitters. Let's say the sign-call house is listed at $250,000 — what I do is look up and pull the best two houses I can find; one for $300,000 and one for $325,000.

That way, when we look over the back fence of the $250,000 sign-call house and see an industrial complex with overflowing garbage bins, or apartments with cars up on blocks, if I do indeed see those things then I'm 100% ready with photos of my cleanup hitters. We're already out and inside the neighborhood, and (are you ready for this?) the chances are *very good* that you will sell them one of your cleanup hitter houses. Here's why: They've just seen what $250,000 will buy them and they are disappointed. They were in a hopeful mood and ready to see something great and buy.

So the sign-call house was a big disappointment. So now you're taking them to a house that, as your research has shown you, has all the amenities they said they wanted *and* it's in the same neighborhood. They've just been emotionally slapped by a sign-call house that had motivated them to get *out and look*. Again, they are in a buying mood and they've just been disappointed.

Unless they ask me, I don't mention that cleanup-hitter house #1 is $300,000. And if they do ask, I say, "It's $300,000, but we are going to offer a lot less!"

Who wouldn't go and take a look? These people are ready to buy and you are going to make it right because in the battle between logic and emotional need, *need* almost always wins the day. Here's what we know about our business: if a buyer looks, a buyer buys. Get them to look and they will absolutely buy!

So this is a very important thing to understand: sign calls are opportunities. *Never* go out to show just one house. Rise up and embrace the opportunity that's been presented to you. But you have to come ready. Have two or even three cleanup-hitter houses ready to show the buyer, because sign-call buyers are motivated buyers. Don't go out unprepared, grumbling about the waste of time. Remember, you get what you expect! I expect to sell a house — or at the very, very, *very* least — I expect to develop a new client PROVIDING they'll do just one more thing for me *before* I rush out to meet them: I *always* ask sign-calls if they've spoken to a lender and whether they are confident in their loan program of choice. If they say

> Have two or even three cleanup-hitter houses ready to show the buyer, because sign-call buyers are motivated buyers.

yes, then I proceed out the door. But if they say no, then I ask them to do a very simple thing: "Will you speak to my best lender for two minutes over the phone?"

They usually will. But if they don't have their loan program in place, and if they won't speak with my lender, then I won't go out to meet them unless they can talk the talk, and assure me that they have $100,000 to put down, along with excellent credit. (I've gotten to the point where their answers to my questions will tell me all I need to know about their qualifications to buy a house.) And if they are at all hesitant to speak with my lender, I tell them that I'll gladly spend an hour or two with them if they'll just give me those two minutes.

That's a fair trade for what is essentially a blind date.

Know *Before* You Go

My hope is that you are reading *Momentum* to help you thrive, which, if I'm doing my job, means that the lessons presented in these pages will help you better utilize your time. Probably the most important lessons I can offer are there to help you learn to maximize your time by improving upon what you already do. You can't add days to the week, so you must find ways to make more money in the same amount of time.

> You can't add days to the week, so you must find ways to make more money in the same amount of time.

Seems easy? Seems obvious? I think so, too. But again and again and again I see agents who take buyers out dozens of times and still come up empty. They *think* they are working hard by beating the streets with buyers to look at houses. Working hard? Okay. But they aren't working smart.

What will your buyer absolutely *not* live without? What will your buyer *potentially* live without? And, lastly, most importantly, can the house be upgraded or added to, because, more often than not, it can be improved and you're just not seeing it.

If you truly want to make more money these are NOT minor concerns. If you show up to a house with a buyer and you don't know the answers to those questions, you are putting the cart before the horse. You are wasting time.

So you have to ask questions. "Do you *really* have to have a pool, or if we find the right house, could we have one put in?" Save yourself time, and make more money *faster* by asking questions, and then challenge yourself to actually *listen* to the answers and incorporate them into your search.

A $300,000 house *without* a pool is going to be a lot nicer home than a $300,000 house with a pool. This makes the sale easier. They can put the pool in *later*. Because square footage, neighborhood, school districts — *these* can and will often be deal breakers. But pools, garage space, flooring, counters, window treatments, landscaping? *These* are opportunities. *These* do not have to break deals.

Stop Emailing Properties to Clients

Can the cart be placed in front of the horse? It can, but why would you do such a thing? Some of you may be having trouble getting buyers to go out and look at properties. You email and email and email — you even call them — but you just can't get to first base working with buyers.

Here are some of my "yes do!" and "no don't!" suggestions.

I almost *never* email buyers photos of a property. I mean that: I almost *never* email a client a property. (Just keep reading!) Second, I *pride* myself on knowing what my buyers want. This goes back to asking questions and getting answers. Ask questions. It saves *them* time, but more importantly, it saves *you* time.

> Do *not* send buyers pages of properties hoping to catch their eye.

Have you flooded a buyer with emailed properties, just hoping for a fortunate hit and an easy sale? If so, DON'T!

Yes, find *and attract* clients in the net of open houses (remember, there's an entire chapter in *Momentum* devoted *entirely* to this art). But once you have them, if you want to work effectively you must change course 180 degrees. You must not shoot every possible property in your buyer's direction. That's right! Use a wide net to attract buyers, followed by a carefully selected presentation of homes for them to choose from.

Do NOT send buyers pages of properties hoping to catch their eye.

First of all, it's lazy and ineffective. As an example, how many jobs have you gotten by posting your resume to a job board? How many spam advertisements do you get per month? Now, how many spam advertisements have you replied to? Blanketing clients with email is a waste of everyone's time. Using the methods outlined here, you've got to take buyers by the hand and show them your five or seven properties in ascending order, from worst to first regardless of geography. Don't flood buyers with everything that crosses your desk. Instead, ask them specific questions and then find them the *right* properties (better to ask too many questions than to show them too many properties). A confused mind freezes *every time*. Find five or seven properties, and then when you are *certain* you have what they are looking for, call them.

Now, on the occasions when you come across a supreme property that you know is right for your client, I recommend that you do the following. Once I've asked my questions, done my research, and know *exactly* what my buyer is looking for — something that will both impress *and* get their juices flowing — I call and say, "Mrs. Buyer, I've found you a great property! It has five acres and is right by the lake. If this were *my* listing I would have gone for $600,000. But it's listed for *only* $550,000 and it just posted 27 minutes ago!" Then to *really* create a sense of urgency, I ask, "Can you get off work right now?"

That's right: to create a sense of urgency for an ideal house, call them at work in the middle of the day and ask if they can meet you right then.

When I have the home-run house right in front of me, I *absolutely* call buyers and ask them if they can get off work. This shows them that it's a big deal — it must be! Who would ask them to get off work for a run-of-the-mill showing?

Not me and certainly not you.

Sometimes the buyer can't get away and that's just the way it is. But more often than not they can't meet me fast enough! Which is smart because if I'm calling them at work it's going to be a great property.

I don't waste their time and I don't waste my time. And I certainly don't flood them with lazy emails of properties. That way, when I call and say, "This is it," they are ready to go.

Most agents ask, "Can you meet me *after* work?" (Or even that weekend.) But if it's a great property and I am 100% certain of its value, I call and ask them to meet me right then.

While I do this regularly (ask buyers if they can get off work), I never do it casually. If I'm going to call a person at their place of business and ask them to meet me, it's because I have that one incredible listing that I know is a perfect 10 and it just can't wait another second.

> To create a sense of urgency for an ideal house, call them at work in the middle of the day and ask if they can meet you right then.

This means I know the area and the price of comparable homes. This means I've done my homework. This means that I know the distance from anything and everything that is *truly* important to the buyer: schools, parks, lakes, freeways, downtown, shopping, etc. This means I know, absolutely KNOW, that comparable houses are going for $600,000 (or whatever they are going for) and that the $550,000 is due to a corporate move or something else that was pressing.

And that's how you get buyers to leave work on short notice: by serving up perfectly prepared filet mignon. When I ask a buyer to leave work to meet me I expect, COMPLETELY AND FULLY EXPECT that my buyer is going to buy that house. I know my client, and I know the property, and we are going to win the lottery. We are going to get that house and there is no time to waste! This isn't hype. This is preparation. And *this* saves you time and makes you money! If I ask a buyer to leave work it creates urgency and expectation. It tells the buyer, "THIS CANNOT WAIT OR YOU WILL MISS OUT!"

Now, sometimes they simply can't break free and then we arrange to see the property at the very first opportunity — usually that evening. But think about it: *this* respect and this level of response *will not happen* when you blanket them with each and every *nearly* acceptable property that comes across your computer screen. So if your method of working with buyers is to flood them with properties and hope that one sticks, then you need to stop that *immediately*.

I have a friend who is in advertising. She also teaches people how to perfect their searches and find the right targets to direct their marketing. She says that whenever anyone first gets into publicity or marketing, one of the biggest, *most common* mistakes they make is to blanket clients with "everything you have in your sales bag" and hope something sticks. Thousands of hours are wasted by emailing people that aren't a good fit for what you are selling and then sending those people who *might* be right nearly everything "just in case one thing catches their eye."

First, spam emails and white-noise conversation *not only* turn people off, they put them on the defensive, which puts them in a bad mood. Blather makes people feel dehumanized.

Second, you don't want to waste your time with the type of buyer who *needs* to see 50 homes to make a decision. That's a waste! If that's who they are then refer them out! (And take your 25% referral fee!)

Third, you don't want to be the type of ineffective agent who sits at his desk and thinks he is working hard just because he electronically forwards property after property to his buyers. This is a huge mistake!

I know people like this. They may mean well, but they are confusing activity with accomplishment — which is an all-too-common error in real estate.

You are a pro; a consummate, hard-working, focused professional. You must know your business, because if you know your business, your clients will listen to you and do exactly what you suggest.

So to repeat: there's a contrast here when you work with buyers. First, you want to *accumulate* buyers as fast as you can by using the wide net that is an open house. But *once a person becomes your client* you *absolutely* want to *completely* change approaches by specifically directing your searches and limiting the houses and properties you will show. Do not send buyers more than a few properties via email. This is not about personal style. This is about effectiveness and how our minds work. Blanketing buyers with properties will only make your job harder and delay sales and lose you clients. Remember, a confused and clouded mind freezes every time!

> **Do not send buyers more than a few properties via email.**

These two divergent tactics (effective open house to accumulate clients *fast*, followed by a *focused* approach when choosing what properties to show buyers to maximize your time) will *quickly* make you money while also earning you a reputation for professionalism and efficiency.

If They Look, They Will Buy

So, you've been working hard with a particular buyer. He came to an open house and told you he was completely ready and qualified to buy a new home and he wanted you to represent him. You asked your questions, found out what he was looking for, and made your list of homes, and now you are ready to find your client a house.

Then, out of the blue — halfway down the road to a sale — the buyer suddenly tells you he wants to wait until summer. And summer is six months away!

Some agents get indignant and say things like, "Are you crazy?! Interest rates are going to be a full point higher by this summer!" They then go on to warn Mr. Buyer that the market is about to explode and that home prices are going to skyrocket.

Bad move.

This is all a big mistake because now it's you against him. The moment you argue with a buyer it becomes a boxing match where nobody wins. Up come the gloves and down go the sales.

What to do when a buyer suddenly stalls? I immediately agree with him! Initially, at least, I don't tell him anything. Not at first. They didn't ask my opinion, so I say, "You want to wait? No problem! I will help you find a home this summer."

After his eyebrows have risen and fallen with surprise, you can feel that his guard has gone down. Maybe he was afraid to tell me that he wanted to wait (and the chances are, he wanted to wait because he felt afraid).

Then I casually say, "In the meantime, to help expedite your search this summer, I've done some research so let's take you out and introduce you to the market. Let's take a couple hours and show you *exactly* what $450,000 buys you." (Or $160,000. Or $230,000, or …) "This way, in the summer you will be more educated on what a good buy is compared to now."

Interest Rates Don't Matter

With the pressure to make a decision off, arranging to go out and look just for "informational purposes" keeps "it" (your business relationship) going. And while you may be thinking that you wanted to tell Mr. Buyer that "interest rates might go up" because you *honestly* believe that they will, that is a mistake. Here's why: in general, interest rates don't matter. People don't buy (or pass on) houses because of interest rates. If a buyer is convinced that waiting is best for him, I don't argue with them. I'm on *their* side. I always want to be on *their* side of the fence, not mine.

> People don't buy houses because of interest rates.

No matter where you are in the process of working with a buyer, I've found variations of the following verbiage to be *extremely* effective in the process of working with someone who unexpectedly puts the brakes on. To keep it going, and to educate them so that *when* they are ready to buy you have them prepared, I say, "Do you have 30 minutes? I want you to get your feet wet. Let me show you two or three of the best houses you can get *right now* in your price range so you have something to compare it to this summer."

If They Look, They Will Buy (Redux)

If you are like me and you sometimes use a yellow highlighter to underline phrases or paragraphs in books or articles, then you'll want to highlight this next part as much as any line in *Momentum*: "IF THEY LOOK, THEY WILL BUY."

Remember, the natural law of real estate says, "If they look, they will buy." By telling you (and, perhaps most importantly, by reassuring themselves) that they are going to wait a month or even six months to buy, then it's your job to *gracefully* get them out

> "If they look, they will buy."

looking. Get buyers out looking at real estate and when they see a house that excites them they will actually move forward with an offer.

Why? Because the pressure's off and there are no expectations. No matter what the industry or product, be it big-screen televisions or a pair of shoes — or even if it's a house — *looking* leads to buying. It's human nature. They're comfortable now because you are not going to push them. YOU *are on* THEIR *side.* They relax and let their guard down and actually enjoy the experience.

Lots of people won't buy *anything* when there's expectation. Looking at houses in this relaxed state of mind is really the best of all worlds. They see the home of their dreams and WHAM! They *have* to have it. If you put a buyer at ease and get them to continue looking, my money's on the best outcome, because if they look, they will buy.

So, your first goal should *always* be to strengthen the relationship by being on the buyer's side. Don't burn bridges. NEVER put your gloves on! Now's the time you put your arm around your buyer's shoulder and walk them into their dream home.

Does this mean your buyer *doesn't* have the right to shop for a house for 6–12 months? Of course not! Mr. Buyer can look as long as he pleases . . . just not with you or me. If they *really* want to be looky-loos, refer them out and collect a 25% referral fee.

But we aren't concerned with those types of clients. We are concerned with buyers who are ready to buy — even if they don't yet know it. So the next time you are arranging your list of five to seven homes to show a client, repeat the following truth to yourself over and over again, and through preparation put yourself in a position to make it happen: *"If they look, they will buy."*

Writing Strategic Offers vs. Traditional Offers

Just about every agent in every region of the country writes 30-day closes. I devote an entire chapter to this ("The Power of the 10-Day Close"), but of course there is a huge crossover between efficiently working with buyers and making certain that *your* buyer gets his house. It's absolutely vital to your success that writing strategic offers be mastered as a way to set yourself apart. Simply, this is where the rubber meets the road on your journey to making more money fast.

Ideally, you want to have so many clients that you can pick and choose whom you are going to work with. I work in "ideals" because I've learned how to turn best-case scenarios into reality.

A down market or a bad economy? There's been a lot of shake-out in real estate, and a lot of agents have left the business. *This* means opportunity. This means a lot of buyers are looking for agents. And if your experience has been a shortage of clients, then I would bet it's a lead-generation problem. And lead-generation problems are solved by holding dynamic open houses.

Ideally, you want to have clients coming and going, at all stages of the buying process, as well as a huge line of what I like to call "uncoachable buyers" that you have farmed out to other agents for your 25%. Remember, you only have time to work with coachable buyers (and sellers, for that matter).

This is good business. This is how you make time *and* real estate work for you.

In real estate you have no such obligation to keep someone who is uncoachable around. But, of course, just like in sports, agents keep uncoachable talent around because it's what they have to work with at the time. In other words, it's all they've got! They figure a tough, grouchy, stubborn buyer who thinks he knows more than the agent is better than having no one to work with at all.

This is wrong-headed thinking and will result in you wasting your time and making less money.

I have learned that having no clients is preferable to having un-coachable ones. Having zero clients will force you to lead-generate (i.e., dynamic open-houses) and find more cooperative clients.

It's a cycle. An agent with a poor lead-generation pattern will accumulate *and hold on to* uncoachable clients who will keep him busy jumping through hoops instead of selling houses to easy-to-work-with clients.

The 10-Day Close: An Introduction

"The Power of the 10-Day Close" is an important chapter in *Momentum* AND in your real estate life. That's because the 10-day close will *exponentially* increase your odds of getting the property for your client, in part, because the other agents will be writing slow, traditional offers. Your goal is to stand out in a way that is effective — and by "effective" I of course mean you must stand out because you have a foolproof method to get your clients the house of their dreams *sure and fast.*

Another reason I introduce "The Power of the 10-Day Close" right here is because much of the introduction of *Momentum* was written to remind you to be open to learning new methods and adapting to changes in our business and our economy. In my business, I use 10-day closes consistently, but I have to admit that, once again, when I initially heard about them, I wondered if it was possible to actually close that fast.

Of course, I don't wonder any more. Ten-day closes flat-out work! And I've done hundreds of them.

I could pull my hair out railing against the 30-day close, but I don't have to. They are still the "norm" for the industry and they still exist because that's the way it has always been done. Nothing more and nothing less.

So with "traditional" 30-day closes in mind, I say ... "coffee" and "want ads."

Coffee is a commodity and want ads are a service. But do they have anything to do with real estate?

Maybe.

Now say "Starbucks" and "Craigslist."

A *lot* different, isn't it? It's a cliché, but it's a cliché because it's true. The founder of Starbucks and the inventor of Craigslist looked at something you see every day — something so ordinary and basic most people likely never even thought about them as having the potential to be changed or to be improved upon (or altered or repackaged). But with a few tweaks, a couple of savvy entrepreneurs changed the way we look at those entities. It's almost as if they reinvented trees or recolored the sky.

For better or for worse, things stay the same until someone figures out a better way. When it comes to working with buyers, look at 10-day closes the same way the creators of Starbucks and

Craigslist looked at coffee* and advertising. They saw things that were almost as common and familiar as night and day, and they put their own spin on them and changed the way we live (and made billions in the process).

Thirty-day escrows are five-cent cups of coffee. Ten-day closes are espresso macchiatos. Thirty-day escrows are pogo sticks. Ten-day closes are rocket packs strapped to your back. History shows again and again that people who are slow to adapt to change get run over and left behind. It's a fact of capitalism that if you don't change and adapt, your business *will* die. Make changes and grow or you'll soon be obsolete.

> **Make changes and grow or you'll soon be obsolete.**

I remember a boss I once had saying that he would never use a fax machine. In fact, he said that faxes were just a business fad and the mail was the only way to send "real" contracts. (He quickly adapted.) They said the same thing about "talkie" movies back in the 20s. "Just a fad."

You get the idea? Pet rocks? Fad. Hula hoop? Fad. Fax machine? Innovation. Ten-day closes?

Innovation.

You want to set yourself apart? You need to innovate and embrace change whenever possible. Embrace the 10-day close and conduct your real estate business with 10-day closes as the norm, *not the exception*, and I can almost guarantee you that your income will drastically increase. As for lenders who say they can't do them, or that they can't be done, I get three calls a week from lenders who plead with me to be a part of *their* machine of 10-day closes. So if you don't think you can find a lender who can close in 10 days, think again! They're out there. Locate them by interviewing lenders and explaining to them that you plan to revamp your business to utilize 10-day closes as the

---

* Remember, at *most* restaurants, cafes, and diners, coffee was a mere nickel when *Starbucks* was founded in 1971, *and refills were often free!*

"norm." If the people you interview aren't interested, move on and find the savvy lenders that are.

These Are Changes *You* Have to Create

So why has most of the real estate industry delayed its move to the 10-day close? Some agents just cannot get their heads around the 10-day close even when my buyers beat their buyers for homes on a daily basis. I love telling the listing agent that my buyer is ready to close in 10 days. I love the head scratching as agents scrunch up their faces, unable to imagine how anyone can close in 10 days. The truth is that ANYONE can close that fast. *Anyone*, that is, who remembers just one thing: You've got to stop letting lenders dictate the speed of *your* business.

> Stop letting lenders dictate the speed of your business.

Because as the man said, "You just have to want it!" You just have to want it AND position yourself with a group of lenders who can rock and roll!

I want you to repeat after me:

My buyers are going to close in 10 days!

My buyers are going to close in 10 days!

MY BUYERS ARE GOING TO CLOSE IN 10 DAYS!

If you will organize your real estate pipeline with people that are ready, willing, and able to do 10-day closes, you will absolutely make more money. The very first time you tell the listing agent to tell the seller that "My buyer is so serious we are ready to close in 10 days," will be the moment a light goes ON inside your head. You'll get that house and that light will never go out.

Now, there's an entire chapter in *Momentum* happily devoted to the nuances of the 10-day close, so I don't want to double up here. I *do* want to introduce a few points. First, I don't tell my buyer about the 10-day close until we are writing an offer on the house they want. Then, if I KNOW they are serious about the purchase, I explain to them that the 10-day close is going to be our "closer." The 10-day close is going to be our walk-off homer. It's going to win us the game.

It's so simple. "My buyer is ready to put proceeds in your seller's pocket in 10 days! Not 30 days! Not 45. Ten days and it's all over!" Imagine the power of a pipeline that offers that inducement as just a regular old part of doing business.

Imagine how much more likely the seller is to accept your offer — even over offers that are higher — because you are willing to close so fast?

It can be that easy.

Because until that house closes escrow it's just a house. But when that house closes escrow, if the seller owes $200,000 on a $400,000 house, he's going to put $200,000 in his pocket *20 days faster* than the competition. Think of the power of that! A 30-day close means 30 days for things to go wrong. When you close in 10 days, that's *at least* 20 days that you're eliminating the possibility of a change of heart. The seller has $200,000 in his pocket 20 days sooner, meaning he's collecting interest, investing, paying off debt *that much more quickly*. If cash is king, then you are royalty, because you are showing the seller the money!

Who Is on *Your* Side to Close Fast?

You already have more allies in closing fast than you realize. The selling agent will be your best friend in fast closes. Three percent of $400,000 is $12,000 you are going to put in his pocket *superfast!* And once you get the selling agent on your side, the deal is practically done! Ask any selling agent, "I know you have three or four other offers, all 30- to 45-day closes. *My* buyer is good to go in 10 days so we all get paid. How would you like to get paid in 10 days, Mrs. Listing Agent?"*

---

* Don't forget to remind the listing agent that by choosing your buyer, HE gets paid fast, and the seller gets proceeds much earlier AND gets to move out *peacefully* a month later with NO STRESS!

Who appears the most serious? Who appears the most ready? Who's going to get that house? My buyer, 99% of the time!

The 10-Day Close: Common Obstacles Revisited

As I cover in Chapter 4, "The Power of the 10-Day Close," there are a few necessary and relatively simple adjustments you must make to your business model to ensure that you overcome the most common obstacles to getting your client a house using the 10-day close. A quick foreshadowing of these:

First, most sellers can't be out of the property in 10 days.

Who cares? You expect this and are actually going to use it to help close the deal, because you are actually going to *give* the seller a month's free rent and 30 days to move out.

Now, occasionally I get a buyer who says, "Why would I give the seller a free month's rent?"

That always makes me laugh. I just tell them about the forest and the trees. I ask Mr. Buyer to consider what he most wants from the transaction? Of course, he usually says, "The house." And, of course, the conversation *usually* ends right there. In a full-blown competition for a desirable property, we are getting Mr. Buyer the house. "Lost rent" of $1,700 is a small price that isn't actually even going to be lost.

Here's why: just remember, when you close in the middle of a month, your first payment isn't even due until the first day of the *following* month. You have 45 days, even more, sometimes, before your first payment is due. If there are no other offers, ask the seller to simply make their normal payment to the buyer instead of the bank. It will cost the seller nothing.

Why Me? Why Not Me?

Remaining married to the old way of doing business just for the sake of keeping the status quo makes me cringe. I love tradition, but when it comes to business I hate old-fashioned thinking. Here's how deals go down for most agents: they are sweating out a 45-day close, and on the 44th day the buyer has a problem with the loan, so the mortgage lender says he needs another two weeks to fix it.

The seller comes back and says, "Look, I'm buying my property. This is going to mess up my rate lock and I'm going to be out $3,000."

Now the seller wants to sue the buyer for $3,000 and everyone is calling their lawyers.

Just about anyone reading this who has been in real estate longer than a year or two knows the frustration of that situation. In fact, it's one of the worst, and most common, setbacks we realtors face. To be involved in that scenario is like being stuck in business quicksand.

Yet while that delay scenario is all too common in real estate, it's also almost entirely avoidable. Because if you close in 10 days and the seller has money in his pocket, then you will find that you all are moving in peace and harmony and seemingly at your leisure.

Be quick, but don't hurry. Ten-day closes are not frantic, down-to-the-wire transactions. *That's* what 30-day closes are. Ten-day closes — quite different from longer closes — happen in the natural rhythm of business. MUCH LESS goes wrong, there are *fewer* delays, and everyone is actually much more in sync than they are with a slow close.

Why don't more agents do 10-day closes? More often than not, it's the mortgage broker who dictates the speed of real estate transactions (pardon me while I take a deep breath). This is entirely unacceptable. This is about teaching mortgage brokers that they do not control the speed of transactions anymore!

> Teach mortgage brokers that they do not control the speed of transactions anymore!

In my business, I have mortgage brokers who start-to-finish can do a loan in five days. *Ten days is twice as long as you need!* Now, I realize not everyone has perfect credit and it might take

30–45 days for some buyers to get their loan. *That's okay.* Ten-day closes are generally for people with 640 FICO scores or better. Your goal *should be* to have so many clients that you only have the time to work with buyers who are easy-loan clients and motivated to move quickly.

Accumulating clients in the pipeline will cure the problem of long closes.

Creaky 17-Day Contingencies

Another age-old real estate tradition that needs to go the way of the dinosaur is 17-day contingencies. Everyone has a 17-day loan contingency. Everyone has a 17-day inspection contingency. Everyone has a 17-day appraisal contingency. (The exact number varies from state to state and even county to county.)

So all of these other offers are coming in and everyone has these long contingency dates in which to back out or have a problem that stops the sale dead in its tracks.

So what about due diligence? *I mean all of it.* How long *should* it take? The inspection? The reviewing? The prelim? The seller disclosures? *Exactly* how long should all this take?

Just about everyone is doing the old 17-day contingency, but we do ours in nine. The reality is that all the contingencies can be completed in nine days for a 10-day close. (You actually need no more than five days to comfortably wrap them all up so, by comparison, nine days is a small eternity!) Seventeen days? Seventeen days just isn't smart and it certainly isn't necessary. And if you insist on keeping your 17 days, you are losing business — because, be warned, someone else is going to hustle and do it in nine days and wipe the mat with you.

We don't want that to happen! But those who say it can't be done are wrong. *Flat wrong!* And, more importantly, they are going to get buried by those who *can and will* do it.

If you want to save time working with buyers, and make more fast money, the 10-day close is one of the most innovative, most modern, most forward-thinking *superweapons* that you'll ever have at your disposal. You're the nose of the missile. You're the captain of the Blue Angels. You are speed and change and in total command. You are no longer just trying to make the system work for you, *now you're making the system your very own!*

Earnest Money Deposits

If you want to make *absolutely certain* that your buyer has the best opportunity to get the house they want, then you must find an edge so that every transaction points directly back at *your buyer* as the most serious option.

How does your buyer get chosen when there's so much noise?

Everyone puts up earnest money deposits. Traditionally, buyers put up 1% of the home's purchase price. So if a house is $300,000, then the buyer puts up $3,000.

Lately, I've been seeing even smaller deposits than the traditional 1%.

What I encourage my buyers to do is to double or even triple the earnest money deposit. I encourage them to come in with $7,000 or even $9,000. Put that money up!

If you are putting 20% down on a $300,000 house, that's $60,000 down! So the earnest money deposit here would traditionally be $3,000 so that the $57,000 balance would be brought in just prior to COE.

I say, put $9,000 in the earnest money deposit, and then I have my buyers bring the balance of $51,000 at COE. While this makes just a small difference to the buyer, it makes a huge difference to the seller.

For contrast, here are examples of other offers: one buyer is giving a $2,500 deposit. The next plunks down $3,000. But *my buyer* is giving $9,000.

Okay. Who appears to be more serious?

Remember, this costs you and your buyer *nothing*. But the appearance of being ultraserious means that your buyer is more likely to get that house. It's that old radio station with the call letters WIFM or "What's In It For Me?"

When the seller sees that much more of a commitment — two or three times as much as the other offers — then human nature takes over and 90% of the time Mr. Seller will choose you!

Again, who would *you* choose? The typical buyer with 3,000 reasons to close escrow or the exceptional buyer with 9,000 reasons to close escrow?

Of course, there's no risk. Your buyer's $9,000 is never at risk because you don't remove the contingencies just because of the 10-day close (although the $3,000 is at risk with a 30-day close).

When there are two or three or ten people clamoring for a property, it's important to have as many edges as possible. By putting more money down, your client appears the most serious. Your client is willing to put three times as much money down on the earnest deposit as the competition. He is going to be ready to close in 10 days, which means that all of the interested parties — the seller, the listing agent, and you — are all going to get paid *much* faster. All that, AND your client is going to let the seller stay in the house for 30 days for *free!*

But this is a competition and I don't just stop there. I don't stop at my superior terms. There are other people to consider. I am *constantly* reminding the listing agent of all those benefits and asking him to clearly explain these benefits to the seller.

There's one more thing I like to do to absolutely *positively* close the deal for my buyer: I take the step of having my loan officer call the listing agent. I do it all the time. I have the loan officer call the listing agent and brag about how great the buyer's credit is and what great secure jobs (provided it's the truth) my buyers have — I make sure they all know the loan is a slam dunk! (Even if it's an FHA buyer.) This talking up my client is the icing on the cake *and* the cherry on top! You have your loan officer call the listing agent and brag, *brag*, BRAG about your client's credit and rave, *rave*, RAVE about your lender's ability to produce loan docs in the next three to five days. (Ninety-nine percent of buyers' agents skip this important step, but not me! And now ... not you, either!)

Even when my buyer is *thousands* of dollars *under* the offers of the 30- and 45-day closers, our *triple money down* earnest-money deposit, *plus* the 10-day close, *plus* 30 days free rent, *plus* my loan officer making a call to the listing agent to brag — *this sequence sets me apart and seals the deal for my buyer almost every single time!*

I also make it a point to remind the listing agent to come back to us with any counteroffer. I may even say, "Forget the other offers and deal exclusively with us. After all, we are the ones who are going to close fast and get you (Mr. Listing Agent) and the seller paid superquick!"

The only thing we may have to do is fix the price. Ask for the counteroffer. Because if we can agree on price, ours is the sweetest offer, *guaranteed!* So I constantly have listing agents return exclusive counteroffers to us (this is control). If we need to come up with $20,000 more, if my client wants the house, we get it! The important thing to remember is that my buyer is in the driver's seat. It's my buyer's choice to take the house or take a pass. This all sure beats highest and best! And you will find your buyer almost always takes the seller's counteroffer. After all, they are the lucky recipient of a home that was so desirable it was the object of a bidding war.

When I was first starting out, I honestly believed that our offers were only as likely to win the house as my client's pockets were deep. In other words, multiple offers meant a bidding war and nothing else. As an inexperienced agent all I could do to compete was have my buyer throw money at every problem. Lots of money. My inexperience cost myself and my clients both money and missed opportunities.

Who to Work With, Who to Avoid

Momentum is all about statistics and averages and playing the odds that YOU create. The Grand Canyon was created over thousands of years by water moving slowly but consistently over solid rock. Being consistent makes all the difference in the world. With that in mind, there are some people in some professions that I hesitate to take on as clients because I have found them to be consistently more difficult to work with than people in other professions. For example, nearly every time that I've worked with an engineer the transaction has gotten painfully slow. Engineers are precise people. They want to know the GPA of the local high school students who go on to attend graduate school. They want to know the degree of slope of the driveway because when they retire in 20 years they are going to buy a fifth wheel and they want the proper angle. God bless 'em! But I don't like working with engineers. I have no patience for their pursuit of nonexistent perfection. I don't eliminate anyone else based only on their career, but of all the unique professions that I've worked with, when I get someone who works as an engineer I almost reflexively farm them out.

> When I get someone who works as an engineer I almost reflexively farm them out.

What if someone is rude to you from the get-go? Give them the heave-ho. Quickly. This may sound like a no-brainer, but we are businesspeople and we like the bird in the hand. Rude client? Let 'em fly away. You don't need it. Simply, if someone is rude or expresses a sense of entitlement right off the bat, then you can expect that they will only behave worse over time. Why are you afraid to take a stand? Do you fear you'll never get another client? First, you are farming the tough nuts out. Referral! You could make a living referring out every single client, but you won't have to. Second, by farming them out early, you free yourself up for additional, easier-to-work-with clients. Again and again and again I have seen that potential clients who are rude are more likely to be unhappy, more likely to complain, more likely to expect the world — and expect *you* to cut your commission — because they feel the world owes them. Never mind why. That's not your problem. It's called the principle of vacuum: get rid of what you don't want in order to make room for what you do want. Replace negative, high-maintenance clients with positive clients.

Rude, unhappy people are even more likely to sue you than clients who can control themselves long enough to at least *act* polite (and rude attorneys are even more likely to sue you because they can sue you for free). So if they are rude, dump 'em! You'll make money in the end from the 25% referral fee.

Internet Leads and Sign-Call Credit Screening (Revisited)

This section is about screening Internet leads and sign calls for viability (when it comes to buying). Whenever I get an Internet lead or a sign call and the caller says, "We found this property on the Internet and we want to see it," I say, "Awesome, I'm on my way."

But before I make that time investment, even before I get off the phone and head out to my car (even before I ask questions which will help me to know EXACTLY what they are looking for AND allow me to find some backup properties), I ask the caller if they've been prequalified for a loan.

If they say, "Yes. Just this week I was approved for this or that amount by this or that bank," or, if they are able to speak about loans and real estate in a manner that lets me know that they've done their due diligence, then I'm on my way out the door.

However, if they say *anything* that leaves it to chance, leaves their financial status a mystery, or even if they are vague, then I tell them that, yes, I'd love to meet them! But first, they have to take two minutes for me and talk to my lender and get prequalified for a loan right over the phone. It takes literally two minutes!

If they can't give that to you, than believe me, it's a mistake to get in the car.

When asked to provide qualifying information, most callers usually say sure.

Let's be frank here: if they're serious *and* qualified, why wouldn't they? We live in an era of identity theft, so some caution is understandable. If there's any hesitation I quickly explain that by providing me with their information they will know their interest rate, their mortgage payment, and the closing costs *in advance*.

That's a valuable thing because I don't want to waste their time, or mine.

There are exceptions to my rules about going out to meet a prospective buyer off an Internet lead. If they talk the talk and assure me that they are willing to put $50,000 down, or if the call comes from a couple, and he's a fireman and she's a career teacher — both at the same jobs for many years — if after a few precise questions I get a good feel for them, then I will usually push ahead and show them the property without first having them speak to my lender.

The opposite remains just as true. When I was new to real estate, I, being Mr. Optimist, would go flying out the door and barreling down the highway for *any call*. (I once forgot to get the address of the place where I was supposed to meet the client.) There I was in my broken-down Chevy, speeding down the road, no idea what the client's financial situation was, but I was on my way to make some money!

One of the best things my parents taught me was to enjoy hard work. But I naively believed just my heading out the door meant that I was working hard, which naturally meant that I was making money.

Truth be told, it was a valuable learning experience that I had to go through to get to a point where I can now quickly tell the difference between who is a viable client and who isn't. Over time, I learned not to swing at that first wild pitch. I learned to work both *hard and smart*, and not just hard.

So while I used to fly out the door at the drop of a hat, obviously, I don't any more. As I've stated again and again and again, *time is money,* and I don't waste either. Spending half your day chasing after clients who could have been eliminated from consideration with a two-minute question-and-answer session is bad business. You aren't being mean by being honest. You are running a business. *Value* your time. Jealously guard it. Complete your due diligence whenever possible and be proud of yourself for being prepared. Don't be emotional. And remember this important point: when it comes to completing your due diligence, it's always possible.

> **When it comes to completing your due diligence, it's always possible.**

But it doesn't end there. I don't blow off buyers with bad credit. Not by a long shot. Instead, if my lender has run the numbers and the caller doesn't qualify, I immediately call the prospective buyer and tell them the truth. I tell them the foreclosure that they had last month will *almost certainly* keep them from qualifying to buy a house *today.*

But just as importantly, I explain to these people that I actually *can* help them find a house. I can help them by getting them into credit counseling or coaching.

Helping someone get their credit together to be able to buy a house — maybe not today, and maybe not next month — but helping them improve their credit to help them buy a house in a year or a year and a half is a very rewarding part of this business. Helping someone who is determined, but who may have just had some bad luck, lost a job, or made some mistakes, *that kind* of helping is one of the best parts of real estate.

My lender gives me their credit score and a rough idea of how long it will take to get their credit in good enough shape to buy a house. That way, when I call the buyer back, I'm not just phoning them with bad news before I blow them off. They gave me their information. They trusted me. So I tell them that with a little work, if they'll just make all their payments for six months, a year, eighteen months, whatever it takes, if they can just be consistent for a specific amount of time, they will *then* be qualified to buy a home.

With just a few minutes of work I've now put these people in my pipeline. With a few minutes of work I've now put these people in line to buy a house.

Here's a sample conversation, because it's never easy telling someone that their credit is bad and that they won't qualify for a loan, so don't! Instead, put a positive spin on it. I say:

"*Congratulations! You've taken an important step. My lender says that in one year you will be qualified to buy a house. Just one year! We all have bumps and bruises on our credit reports. But it's nothing we can't fix,* AND I CAN HELP YOU. *If you'd like some help improving your credit score, my loan officer is an expert at credit repair.*"

This is fantastic! This is great news! Instead of making them feel like miners trapped alone underground, I help them see what might be the first light they've seen in a long time!

I have *never* had a buyer say no to the help.

Be positive, and offer to provide the help they need, and you will both win. Emphasize the fact that they will be able to get a house in a very short period of time, and that you have the person who can help show them the way. Once you've agreed to put them in touch with your credit coach, *then* ask them if they know anyone else (referrals are an incredible way to get new clients — and you are always searching) who is looking to buy or sell.

You're helping them, and as often as not, they'll help you find clients. Then, a year or two down the line, the phone will ring and it will be the couple with the rebuilt credit, recent graduates of credit coaching armed with a whole new outlook and endless possibilities.

TWO
TWO

Dynamic, Powerful Open Houses

Here's a question: when was the last time you added 27 buyers and 4 sellers to your client list in a four-hour period? Has it been a little while? Or has that actually *never* happened for you?

I implore you *not* to be one of those people who can't believe something just because you've never done it. A little cynicism is fine, but not in this case. Because adding over 20 clients in a single afternoon is *exactly* what ONE good open house can do for you! They can turn your business on its ear in a single day.

So if you're saying, "Twenty-seven buyers? Don't you mean 27 *prospective* buyers?" the answer is, "*No!* I don't mean *27 prospective buyers.*" In several words, what I mean is *exactly* what I said. If you execute open houses with a beginning, a middle, and an end plan, then you can absolutely add as many as 30 buyers and as many as 7 sellers in as little as four hours.

And listen to this: I don't care what your market is. Shall I repeat that? *I do not care what your market is!* (Or what your market isn't.)

I mean what I've said here because it's what I do. At one open house I actually added 37 *serious buyers* who planned on pulling the trigger within the next six months, not to mention, that of those 37 serious buyers, 14 or 15 were "right now" buyers — as in, they were ready to buy that day.

Oh, don't remind me. You don't do open houses. You say that open houses don't work. And besides, why waste your time on friendly people, people who click with you, who look into your eyes, shake your hand, AND who are 100% willing to entrust you with their social security number and their private financial information?

You're in real estate. Why would you bother with that?

You can always go back to pay-per-click leads! Searching the Internet for people you haven't met and will probably never meet. If that's your choice, then go ahead and work on those some more.

Let me make what we are going to learn in this chapter perfectly clear: open houses, properly done, can be worth $20,000 to even $100,000 — or more — per day.

> **Open houses can be worth $20,000 to even $100,000 — or more — per day.**

On a recent afternoon I picked up nine buyers in two hours with an average sale price of $500,000. In other words, one open house produced nine buyers who, *combined*, earned me $135,000 in commissions. Not bad for half a day's work!

And let me repeat something else: I don't care what market you are in, because the chances are pretty good that it's not any worse than our market in Sacramento, California.

It absolutely shocks me when I hear about agents who don't bother with open houses. And for those agents who do hold them? I'm equally amazed by how many admit to putting almost zero energy into them. They rush to get there, throw out a few signs, then sit back, open a book, and wait to go home.

Open houses? It's time to begin again. This is Real Estate 101 and class is in session. Open houses? Most realtors hate them! They hate them for a variety of reasons having to do with posting signs, the unknown, boredom, waiting around, and the possibility of rejection.

Well, here's a revelation about me and open houses: I built my career on them. That's right! Where the older agents saw burdens, I saw opportunities, and I 100% honest-to-goodness love them! In fact, it's not a stretch to say that I've had many of my best (i.e., most lucrative) moments selling real estate during open houses. And so when my agents or associates refer to me as the "Open House King," *I love it!*

If you aren't holding dynamic open houses then you are wasting one of the fastest career-building assets that you have going for you.

And that's a shame. It's a shame because, unlike building a team of agents or mastering 10-day closes, both of which take time to implement, *increasing* your business through dynamic open houses is fast and easy and *almost* immediate. Unlike building a team or cultivating 10-day closes, you can improve your sales and increase your income *this weekend* simply by changing your approach (and your attitude) — and best of all you can have fun doing it!

> If you aren't holding dynamic open houses then you are wasting one of the fastest career-building assets that you have going for you.

An Opportunity to Sell Is an Opportunity to Make Money (Or Had You Forgotten?)

I once had a friend who ran his own company in an industry *totally* unrelated to real estate. In fact, this friend had a job title that I always wanted: consultant. I always thought that anyone with a title like "consultant" must have it all figured out.

One day I was listening to my friend talk to a prospective client on the phone. Later that night we were at an event, very low-key, and he was casually working the room, talking to everyone, gathering information and improving his connections.

My friend knew his business well and was confident in his ability. After this event, we were walking out to the car and it dawned on me that my friend wasn't *really* a consultant at all.

In fact, he wasn't a president, and he wasn't a chairman of the board, either.

I'd always considered what he did for a living to be what his title was: consultant. I figured he told professionals in his industry what to do and how to do it for an hourly fee. But that day (I have to admit, I was a little embarrassed by this) I realized that my friend the consultant was *actually* a salesman. I turned to him right then, right there in the parking lot, and I asked him to estimate what percentage of what he did was *actually* sales.

Knowing what I had learned, it was a silly question, and he looked at me as if I were kidding around. "One hundred percent," he said. "It's *all* sales."

In great detail, my friend then went on to explain to me just how much he respected good salespeople and how much time he allotted, not just each year, but *each and every week*, to taking sales seminars or practicing his presentations in front of the mirror. He even told me how frustrated he got when someone was trying to sell him something, but either they weren't very good at it or they hadn't committed to the art of actually selling the product.

Mastery!

I was shocked! My friend was a salesman. But even more interesting was the very simple product he spent his time selling: himself.

From that moment on I saw sales, and my friend, in an entirely different light.

Again: It's Sales — So Take Advantage of Each and Every Sales and Networking Opportunity!

Open houses are premier selling opportunities, but they are also very visible selling and marketing opportunities. You have a product to sell. You have yourself to sell. You have your business to sell. You go there and greet potential clients and everything's up to you. You may feel exposed and naked to the world, but you are surrounded by your product.

Every one of us shops in retail stores. And every retail store has both subtle and not-so-subtle mechanisms to hook us, to get us to notice what they're selling. Thousands of dollars and hundreds of personnel-hours go into getting us interested in what they want us to buy. To do this, stores hire expensive marketing firms to help them display their goods.

Now don't be mistaken. I'm not even talking about the color of the product label, or even the font and size of the words on that label. Millions of dollars go into designing those, as well. I'm merely talking about the *positioning* of the product. I'm referring to the color of the sign that alerts you to that product. I'm talking about the little placard that says "special," and tells you that for $9.99 you can have the deal of your life.

And in response to that marketing, we buy those deals again and again and again. We buy them because we notice them. We buy them *in spite* of ourselves. We buy them even when they are unfamiliar to us, and even sometimes when we like the taste of a different brand better. We buy them because they tell us to. But as much as anything? We buy them because those signs work!

At every level of sales and advertising, investing in the nuances of presentation has been proven to pay off again and again and again in increased volume. Signs that say "Look at me!" actually do get us to look. And getting you to look is the first *and most important* part of the sale. *Incredibly*, it's the most important part of the sale because, as I'll say many times throughout *Momentum*, if they look, they will buy.

And that's one of the most important and key points of selling: get them to look and they will buy.

Now you may think real estate is different from what they do at Whole Foods, but you'd be mistaken. You'd be wrong in lots of ways, but you'd be especially mistaken when it comes to open houses. Because "throwing it together" when it comes to open houses is like driving a high-performance car and then not using the fifth gear.

So for the sake of improving your career and improving your

> **Open houses are the *easiest and fastest* way to increase your income.**

industry knowledge, attempt to read the rest of this chapter with an open mind. Let yourself be taught something new or unfamiliar. Because if you will just give what I'm teaching here a chance, and then give it a try, I promise you that of *all* the information I've chosen to include in *Momentum,* open houses are the *easiest and fastest* way to increase your income and give your business a giant and immediate bounce.

There's So Much More to Open Houses Than *Just* Open Houses

To be sure, open houses are a *major* selling opportunity. But best of all, they are not just an opportunity to sell the house you are showing, but an inroad and opportunity to accumulate clients, gather information, and increase your sales for months and even years going forward.

But you've got to have a plan. You've got to have a system.

It is my goal that as you read *Momentum* your knowledge of real estate will not only expand but also sharpen. I want you razor-sharp and slippery with an easy-to-implement system. But you've got to be willing to adapt. We all sometimes miss the forest for the trees. But to hone your business model you may first need to look inward at your willingness to learn. You need to see the familiar in a new light and from a different angle. If you can do that, then I can reshape and re-energize how you go about the various facets of building your career and increasing your income. Because in *any* economy, with the competition you face in the marketplace these days, you simply can't afford to go through the motions and hope to be successful. *You can't do it!* There are many steps on the road to real estate success that even experienced, conscientious agents ignore or take for granted. Good markets make us lazy, and many of us have gotten sloppy. I understand. We can't be everywhere. We can't do everything. Something that was working just a few years ago (just answering the phone in a booming economy) isn't working anymore. So you've got to grow, or maybe even start again. Because if you haven't mastered the easier, *more accessible* steps to real estate success, it'll be that much tougher to master the more complicated ones.

We're going to change bad habits, start good new ones, and you are going to rock and roll at a level you have previously only dreamt about. Because if you are going to take your business to that next level, or *maintain* your business in good times and bad, you simply can't afford to leave anything to chance. You can't afford to overlook something that is so simple, yet so vital, to your success.

> **You need to learn how to host dynamic open houses.**

You need to learn how to host dynamic open houses. Which means many of you need to start again. And *right here* is that restart line:

Restart Line for Agents Ready to Improve

1. On your mark — you bought *Momentum*
2. Get set — you're reading it!
3. Go! — applying what you've learned

Signage Here, Signage There, Signage Everywhere

Have you ever heard of the purple cow? A guy was in Europe on vacation driving through the countryside. He kept seeing cows that looked the same. Mile after mile after mile, cow after cow after cow, everyone he saw looked *exactly* the same. Bored, he began to wonder, "What if I drove over the next hill and instead of brown and white cows, what if I saw a purple cow?" Then he laughed to himself, "I bet there'd be a thousand tourists standing out there taking pictures." (I'd be right out front.)

The point is that to stand out in marketing, you have to be different. Because *being different* doesn't just make you stand out from the competition — which of course it does do, and which has its own benefits — but being *different* actually attracts people, because people are bored by what's common. People in our business, people in every business, have been lulled to sleep by the status quo.

You've got to be different and you've got to make your open houses look unique to make this work. And I'm not talking about a two-headed purple cow here. (Although, if you hear of one ...) I'm talking about tweaking the status quo. I'm talking about reinventing the familiar. Because if you've driven by an Open House sign recently, you know right now that different isn't all that hard to achieve.

You're on a family vacation. You are driving from California to Arizona, and you are in the middle of the desert. Along about Death Valley, you see a sign that says "Watermelon: 10¢ a Pound."

Does that even really register? Watermelon on sale for ... something. So what?

"So what?" you think. "Watermelons are heavy. What if I drop it on my foot?" You have no idea what a good deal on watermelon is, anyway.

But 10 seconds later you see a sign that says "Strawberries: Two Baskets for $1." You think to yourself, "I like strawberries." Big, bright, red strawberries sure taste good. But then you let yourself forget about it. You're in a hurry to get where you're going. The *real* fun, you think, won't begin until you get to wherever it is that you're headed. The trip itself, you think, is just a drag.

You start noticing cactus and how the pavement up ahead sort of looks like it's covered in water. You've forgotten all about fruit. You've forgotten all about watermelons and strawberries — that is, until a little while later when you notice a sign that says, "Cantaloupes: 30¢ a Pound."

All around you is dirt and sun and cactus. You wonder, "How they'd get all that fruit out here?" Who picked it? Where'd it grow? You're still wondering how they got that fruit out in the middle of the desert, when you see *another* sign that says "Fuji Apples: 19¢ a Pound."

Now your mouth is watering. (My mouth is watering just writing this.) Are Fuji apples red? Or are they green or maybe yellow? You are actually scanning the horizon — and the side of the road — looking for the fruit stand so you can . . .

Okay . . . you're not *quite* ready to stop. Not yet. Oh . . . Okay . . . *maybe* if there's also a gas station you'll pull over. Then you think, "Fruit is good for you." You remind yourself that you should eat more fruit.

You pass another sign and then another. And then another. Where is that darn stand?

By about the 10th or 11th sign advertising fruit you start to realize that you are actually craving some. You drive a little faster. A juicy watermelon slice or a piece of cantaloupe might be just ahead. You're not really in *that* much of a hurry to get to where you're going. The thought of the juice dripping down your chin out here in the middle of the desert sounds kind of cool. Sounds like it just might be the best way to kick off this little trip. After all, it's *your time* now.

Another sign: "Blueberries." And where minutes before fruit was the furthest thing from your mind, now you want some. Now you are desperate for it. Now you are looking for that little fruit stand, hoping it's not a mirage. *Fruit* is now the goal! Is *that* the stand *there?* Is that it? Where is it? Juicy, nutritious, delicious fruit! *You've got to have it!*

Think open houses are any different? Think again. In fact, the desire to possess something may be even stronger with things like homes and cars — big-ticket items — *especially* when you are in the market for them (or aren't overly thrilled with your current model).

Back to fruit. Finally you come upon the fruit stand and there's no stopping you. You veer right and cut off a trucker and steer the car over to the side of the road — dust billowing up from beneath your tires. You jump out of the car and hurry to the displays. You are buying fruit like it's going out of style. Two of those. Two of those. One of those. *Now you're an expert on fruit!* You are buying more than you could ever eat in a single day. You are buying it because it was suggested to you not once, not twice, not three times, but four, five, six times. You've had fruit before. It's good for you! It tastes great! It's fun to say "Yes!" It's fun to have what you want.

This actually happened to my wife and me. We found ourselves driving along the coast devouring fruit like we'd discovered a magic food that would help us live forever.

I'll never forget that fruit stand. And I'm sort of embarrassed about it, but I learned something valuable that day. I learned about the power of signage.

And this *exact same strategy* is the first *and second* lesson to apply to open houses. The first lesson is you need enthusiasm, and that enthusiasm is going to help you relearn something you thought you already knew. And if that enthusiasm is created by pretending that you've never done an open house before, then so be it! Play along, because there's a lot more to this than just enthusiasm.

The second lesson is that you need *serious* signage. If you invest in serious signage, you have begun to change and improve your open houses, and you have begun to say "Yes!" to making more money.

But if you say "Signage, so what?" then you are missing the point. Because I'll bet that 90% of you have never put out more than six signs for an open house — and I'm here to explain to you that six signs just will not do. Not for what I'm teaching. I'm *begging you* to try something. I'm challenging you to put out 25 signs at your next open house. *Do it!* I'm telling you to invest in signage and to put those signs out in every direction until you have *thoroughly* blanketed the area so that *every* approach and each major street has signs advertising your open house. Remember: if you put six signs out, you'll get a "six sign" result.

> **If you commit to 25 signs, you are taking a very important first step towards hosting dynamic open houses.**

But if you commit to 25 signs, you are taking a very important first step towards hosting dynamic open houses — and the best is yet to come!

When and Where for Signs

Sometimes I'll see a sign for an open house in my neighborhood and then I'll notice as I drive toward the freeway or the mall that there are no other signs. *Just one sign on a quiet, residential street?* (Sarcasm alert here!) That solitary sign is certainly going to reel them in!

One sign? That is a recipe for failure! That realtor just isn't trying.

Here's what you do: find the streets approaching the busiest intersections up to and running even more than two miles away from the property and start placing open house signs. Place the signs a good distance in front of these intersections so that you have time to introduce the buyer to the idea that there is going to be something desirable for sale. Signs intentionally placed to start them thinking about your product and to get their desire cravings going good and flowing strong (about 100 yards apart for 400–500 yards as you approach a major intersection).

Then place directional signs just before and also *at* the intersection.

If you are justifiably wondering how much money I have invested in signs, it's a pittance when you consider my hourly wage or the return the signs have given me on my open houses. In fact, it's a steal! I'm saying bite the bullet and invest $300 in signs and you will make tens of thousands of dollars, in part, because of that tiny investment. (As an example, for around $280 you can get 25 impressive-looking custom Coroplast signs with iron legs.)

How many realtors run open house signs for five miles? I know I do. I know my agents do. And I know how well it works. I've had hundreds of people who weren't in the market for a new house come to my open houses because of my signs. I've had people say, "All those signs, you're crazy!" to which I say, "I know, isn't it great!" Many of these people say that they will be looking for a house soon and they want me to represent them. Proudly, I've sold houses to many of those same people because they see what I'm doing for my clients. They see the energy and attention. And they meet me and know that I will do everything I can to help them sell or find a home.

When you hold an open house you want to create energy. Look at Black Friday, the day after Thanksgiving. Let's be honest: When was the last time you were shopping at the mall and they didn't have what you wanted? Probably never! They always do. In my opinion, the best deals are actually the day just *before* Christmas. But the day after Thanksgiving, Black Friday, it creates a buzz and people just *have* to be part of the buying buzz. They wake up at 4:00 a.m. (or stay up all night) to go stand in line outside the mall or Best Buy.

You want to create that buzz with your open houses, and signage is the first vital step to creating that all-important *wow!* factor. You want people walking up to the house. You want people walking away from the house. You want people snapping pictures. When prospective buyers arrive, you want them to see the buzz, notice the activity, and get caught up in the interest. You want them to feel that something important is happening and that if they don't get involved, they will miss out. You want them to feel the momentum and be desperate to be a part of it.

For me, a bad open house draws 20 people. Typically, I get 70–100 people. People in the front yard, people in the backyard, people coming and going. And yet I do *not* advertise in the newspaper. Pure and simple, it's just the signs! (And, as you will soon learn, the draw is also actually what is *written* on my signs, as well.)

Does this sound like the open houses you are used to? Does this sound like I would have time to sit back and read a novel? *These are events!* And I make 100% certain that I meet everyone who walks through the door.

No, it doesn't take a mere five minutes for me to put my signs out. It takes 45 minutes. Nine times the effort equals nine times the result! I look at each and every sign as a sales tool that is working for me. *Representing me!* My little army of signs. I love them! They work for me and they don't take a lunch break and they *never* call in sick!

At my open houses I'm making connections and building a client base. I'm building momentum. I'm building my business. *Strangers*, recruited by my signs, are coming up to me and helping to make me money and build my business.

It's taken me years to learn all that I have about real estate. But right from the start I saw the value of open houses. When no one else wanted to do them, I jumped at the chance and turned them into events.

After my career grew and I needed help with all the open houses I was staging, but

> A full 50% of the people who attend my open houses come for one simple reason: because my signage says "free list of area homes."

before I'd built a team, I actually had my wife work with me. We had so many weekends with more than one open house that I hired an 18-year-old, middle-linebacker type named Eli to manage my sign placement. I briefed this kid on how important open houses were for my business and my family. I explained that I wanted him to be creative with the sign placement, but that I also wanted him to take his time and think about the angle and location of each sign. For $10 an hour Eli helped funnel hundreds and even thousands of prospective buyers into my open houses. And after he had finished placing the signs, I had big Eli act as my wife's bodyguard for the duration of the day. So for $40–$50 dollars, my wife was safe, my signs were placed so that I could run two open houses at once, and best of all, those houses sold *and* I gathered valuable information and accumulated clients. They were events. And to this day I feel that the $10 an hour I spent on Eli was some of the best money I've spent in my life! (Right after the fruit from that fruit stand.)

It's all about investing in yourself and your business. Throughout *Momentum* I use clichés like "Don't be penny-wise and pound-foolish." Open houses, 10-day closes, hiring staff, building a team — I know what it's like to not have any money in the bank. None. Success can seem far off. But I also know that if you are committed to success, better to go without a little something today so that you'll never have to go without it again. Spend the money where and when it matters. And signage matters! It matters *big time!* Signage will make or break your open house, so spend some money on them, and spend the time to place them well. Place them everywhere. You will be shocked at the response that this simple act generates.

Get them and use them.

Planning and Preparing for Your Open Houses: What Your Signs *Must* Say

You need 25 *unique* open house signs. Not 5 signs, not 10, and not 15. You need 25! You need to take these signs out two, three, even five miles to tap into the main traffic arteries. On weekends there are thousands of people driving around looking for things to do. Or they are shopping, and we real estate agents *love* people who are in shopping mode. Get those signs out all the way to the main traffic arteries and if that means five miles, then do it!

The first thing I make certain that my signs say is "Bank Repo." And if you caught that, you are 100% correct: 90% of my open houses are bank repos! Not all, but most. That's 25 signs that say "Bank Repo." The reason is simple: "Bank Repo" means "opportunity." Bank repo means a deal is in the offing. Wounded fish. Blood in the water. And I long ago learned that

25 signs worked best. Yes, 25 will have some redundancy, but that is *exactly* what you want. You must never again settle for an open house that isn't absolutely buzzing with clients — and the combination of 25 signs that scream "Bank Repo" will pack them in! Buyers *and* browsers (i.e., future clients) are more interested in bank repos than simple open houses.

But my signs don't stop at "Bank Repo." To get people to attend my open houses, my signs say, not one, but three important things:

1. Bank Repo
2. Open House
3. Free List of Area Homes

First, it's an open house. "Open House" is the announcement. People who are in the market (and some who are simply curious) come to open houses to take a peek. Second, it's a bank repo. Bank repos cause a lot of interest. They are big draws with lots of excitement. A bank repo means a great deal is a given, and no one wants to miss out on the deal of the century. But third — and this is my absolute closer — is the free list of area homes. *I cannot overstate this*: a full 50% of the people who attend my open houses come for one simple reason: because my signage says "free list of area homes."*

Of the people who attend one of my open houses, 10% are people who just saw the sign and wanted to take a look.

Approximately 40% of the attendees come through the door because it's a bank repo. When I draw 50 people to an open house, 20 of them are there because of the bank repo angle. Free list of area houses? Half! Twenty-five out of 50 people attend

---

* Remember, selling the house is only a part of the open house plan. You are holding the open house to accumulate clients for today, tomorrow, and on into the future. That means you must do everything you can to create a buzz that brings people in!

Make it easy for buyers to find your open houses.

Use a prequalification form like this one at your open houses.

primarily because of that free list — and that 50% creates the biggest buzz and biggest word of mouth, which leads to huge numbers. And make no mistake, it's a numbers game! The more times you come to bat, the more hits you're going to get.

Gathering Information

After you've made a commitment to open house signage that gets people's attention, your next goal is to gather information. *This is incredibly important*: have professionally printed 5×7 applications that say "Keller Williams," "Coldwell Banker," "RE/ MAX", or whatever brand you are with (if you have a brand), or whatever your firm is called. And this part is also very important: *make sure the application has a logo on it.*

Now, I can already hear some of the more analytical agents seeing that form and saying, "A small form like that isn't specific enough."

Remember? First-time eyes? Starting new? Give the notion of comprehensive credit applications a rest, because those will not work for our purposes. In fact, a long form would actually work *against* us. Not *only* is 5×7 specific enough, it's *exactly* the right size. You don't need to know about alimony income, child support, IRS taxes, etc. *Not here. Not now.* DON'T CHANGE THIS FORM!

Human nature. Time. Energy. Suspicion. This smallish form helps to alleviate any and all concerns because you are asking just enough to get what you need, but not so much that you are going to irritate *most people* (and by "most people" I mean people who either are or *might be* in the market for a new house). You want a small, unintimidating form with a line for name and address, occupation, years at present employment, gross monthly income and gross annual income, social security, authorization to pull credit, and a signature. *That's all!*

I CANNOT overstate these two points enough. *First, keep the form short, and second, make sure you have your company's logo on it.* It's simple: the lenders can gather additional information later, and adding the logo is just enough to ensure legitimacy. Duplicate, don't innovate. Once you are a huge success (i.e., you have sold 100+ homes doing this), *then* feel free to tweak it to your location and clientele. But don't change it out of the gate and then say, "It doesn't work." If you do it this way it will work a large percentage of the time. I've tried dozens of forms of various lengths and complexity. I've done the legwork for you. This one works. This is the way to roll!

> First, keep the form short, and second, make sure you have your company's logo on it.

Now, I leave the bottom half of the 5×7 application blank. I do this because a big part of the process revolves around me saying, "Have you heard of the First-Time Home Buyer's Program that we are promoting here at Keller Williams?" (Or Prudential, or Coldwell Banker, or Century 21, etc.)

This is where I tell the prospective client, who has found the open house because of signage, that for somewhere around 4.7% (4.7% as of mid 2011 — but it's been as low as 3.9%) we can put them in a new home. It takes about *one minute* to fill out this application — and I explain to them that in this one minute we can accomplish everything they'd accomplish if they spent an entire hour with a mortgage broker. We all know that if they were to call a mortgage lender, that lender would want them to come down and fill out forms. Lots of forms. The lender would also want bank statements, pay stubs, and W-2s. It's a hassle and a pain and a huge bother, especially when a curious couple is in Saturday-afternoon house-sightseeing mode! Take one minute and be done! No hassles. Fast and easy and totally convenient!

Then I tell the client about the ease of our approval department at my company (or whatever firm you are with). I tell them how our approval department is one of the most liberal, generous approval departments in the world. It's like buying a house at Costco, and our rates are the lowest in the country.

Maybe they ask, "Why are your rates so low?"

Because we are huge and we do this all the time (your approval department is whichever lender you choose to work with).

Everyone Gets Approved!

Honestly.

After someone fills out one of my mini-applications, then I immediately tell them that I will call them Monday with their approval. I *never* say "I will call you Monday to tell you *if* you've been approved." No. It's "I'll call you Monday *with* your approval." It's that fast! It's that easy!

Then I have the lender run the application, which can result in a couple of different scenarios. First, an easy one: let's say it comes back 740 FICO, blended FICO score is 715. He's a California Highway Patrolman, she's a nurse, and they make $125,000 a year and could easily buy a house for $350,000. As we all know, anything in the 700s is outstanding, so that's easy and we can approve them fast. I know the programs the state of California has for police officers (or for nurses) so I call the applicants and tell them that they've been approved and then I prepare to show them prospective properties (along with any perks and special programs that their respective employments may help them qualify for).

Let's pick a tough one. Let's say a couple has a FICO score of 510. We all know that's not a very good score. Most lenders laugh it off and say that maybe they could buy a used car or bag of potato chips, but not a house. If that happens, most realtors have to call and say, "I'm sorry, but you didn't qualify."

Not me. *Never me!*

Let's say the prospective clients with the 510 FICO score are named Bob and Judy. I'm actually going to help Bob and Judy buy a house. I ask my lender, "What if Bob and Judy get it together and start paying their bills on time? When can they qualify?"

Then my lender tells me that if Bob and Judy start paying

their bills on time for 12 months (or whatever amount of time he calculates), they can get approved. I begin to frame it in my mind. Just one year of vigilance and they can buy a house! So I call Bob and Judy and tell them they've been approved to buy a house in 12 months, they just need to make their payments on time. Just 12 months! I'm that specific and I let Bob and Judy know that we are in it together!

That's important. No rejection. Instead, I have provided them with a plan *and* a promise that I am going to help them.

Now, besides the fact that most people who have had credit problems *greatly* benefit from having a clear goal, they now know that someone's in their corner and going to be there when they are ready to purchase. So how do I *prove* that I'm in their corner? I take it all a step further. I get them into credit coaching. Sometimes over the phone in a three-way call with a counselor, sometimes in person, and sometimes just by referral, but I *always* get them in touch with my lender. This way, when Bob and Judy are ready to buy, they know that it was me who helped get them in a position to buy. (To ensure the cycle, my lender always leads them back to me.)

It's absolutely thrilling to see the transformation of people like Bob and Judy. Most couples who can't get approved today can get approved in six months (or so) with a little bit of work, and I love setting them up with a credit coach to make sure we see it through (once again, always use your lender for this).

I cannot easily count all the couples that I have helped this way. And the best part is that they feel as though I did it for them. They are usually extremely grateful (even giddy) and the feeling is that we have formed a bond. It's an incredible experience when a couple shows up at my office ready to buy after improving their credit scores through my lender.

All you experienced agents know that there are only so many people with 740 credit scores. And you must realize that if you are *only* willing to put work into people with perfect credit, then you are severely limiting yourself to a very competitive, select few *potential* clients. But if you can set up your system to work with virtually anyone — and I mean ANYONE with the potential to be a client — you will *substantially* increase your income and your client base!

That signage that brought you 100 people? You're setting yourself up and accumulating buyers and sellers that will stretch out into the future for months or even years. And it's just one open house! And all this is supplemented by a simple credit form that is acquired through dynamic open houses. Every action is related and connected and you must think in terms of the steps it takes to build your business foundation and increase your income. In this chapter, everything up to this point, all this information, is the result of embracing open houses and making them dynamic. Remember, you don't have nearly the connections and possibilities you have if you don't hold open houses that work.

So I call Bob and Judy and I tell them that we will be able to approve them if they are just willing to work on their credit. And let me tell you, virtually none of these people is anything short of excited by the prospect of having someone take an interest in them building their credit because, for the most part, these people have been abandoned by commerce and financial institutions. I've made a lot of money helping these people help themselves, and we both benefit from the process. It's the proverbial win-win, and it hardly takes any time.

I ask Bob and Judy if I can have Joe from the lender call them to give them some credit coaching with the understanding that they can get approved and get into the house of their dreams with just a little work — and they won't be going it alone. We will work with them! Hold their hand. Guide them every step of the way!

I'm always upbeat and I'm always encouraging. I approve everyone with a time frame based on their individual circumstance. And, once again, these folks appreciate the help because so many of them feel isolated and frustrated and alone. They are so grateful for the help that they naturally want to introduce me to other folks, some with great credit, some who themselves need coaching, but the energy and positivity and hope that I put into these relationships pays off many times over, and it helps a lot of people — all this from what so many other realtors would write off as a bad lead.

It's really human nature. The word "approval" is a positive word. People light up when they hear it — and just the idea that they will make progress and achieve their dreams if they simply follow a system that is outlined by a professional credit coach is more than enough for most of these people to work towards buying a house. They can see that there's light at the end of the tunnel. They are excited someone has taken an interest who can help them achieve a goal that they thought was out of reach.

So, you have your 25 signs and you're spending 30 to 45 minutes putting them out and in return for your effort you get *at least* 30 people — but as many as 90 people — who show up for your open houses. You have your applications ready, and these applications lead to clients in the short term and — don't underestimate the referrals that these people will give you — in the long term, as well.

It's extremely important you utilize these open houses to emphasize the fact that *anyone* can take advantage of the first-time homebuyer programs. *Anyone.* These programs are liberal and generous and give them real hope. Work with the best loan officers you can find. Don't ever assume you have the most aggressive, out-of-the-box-thinking loan officers. Great loan officers are one in 100! Find them! Search them out! Ask for referrals from the top agents. Interview and find the right fits and make them work for you!

You Want Out-of-the-Box Thinking? Here's a Shocker!

Here's something I do that very often causes mouths to drop: *If I need more clients, I hold open houses on other agent's properties.* That's right. First, I'll only do it if the house is vacant. I'll call the firm and ask about the house on, say, Oak Valley Road. I ask them if I can hold an open house at that location.

Some listing agents say "Yes!" and some say no. I don't care about the nos — I'm interested in the "Yes!" agents. They are spending time and money trying to sell that house. The owner is breathing down their neck, so the listing agent is actually excited to have me increase the house's exposure. And I'm helping to get the listing agent off the hook for an open house that weekend — now he or she can play while I accumulate clients and make money!

> If I need more clients, I hold open houses on other agent's properties.

I have sold numerous houses this way and the great part is that you can cherry-pick the best properties in the best locations. You are looking for location first and curb-appeal second. The price actually DOES NOT matter, because you are there to build your business.

For a Beginner Falling from a Plane

Here's what I would do if for some reason I parachuted from a plane into a strange city: I would check the system and find the best properties and call the agents and hold open houses in the agreeable-agent's listings. No matter where I fell, there's absolutely nothing else I would need to do to start making a living — and it's all based on open houses which *I know* are the easiest and fastest way to not only start earning a living but also begin to build a business for the long term. You can't unlearn how to ride a bike and once you learn how to hold *dynamic* open houses, you can't *unlearn* that valuable skill, either. (And why would you ever want to?) You will see that the public is not your enemy. These five simple steps:

1. See open houses in a new light.
2. Have enthusiasm.
3. Put out 25 signs.
4. Provide 5×7 applications.
5. Approve *everyone!*

These simple, incredible, wonderful, and easy-to-learn steps will create your foundation of success faster than any other method you can use. So embrace dynamic open houses and make more money faster. And while you're at it, stop and eat some fruit along the way!

THREE

THREE

THREE

THREE

How to Win in Multiple-Offer Situations Almost Every Time

I'm going to start this chapter in reverse by writing about a problem that jumps up and surprises many agents. Here's a common situation for new agents: They go out with a client who *absolutely loves* a house and wants to make an offer. The new agent calls the listing agent and asks, "Do you have any offers on the property?"

The listing agent says, "Nope, none!"

The new agent is understandably excited because he thinks that zero offers automatically mean that *his* client will end up with the house. It's all going to happen! The path is clear! The now-beaming new agent hangs up the phone and *immediately* calls his buyer to communicate that there are no offers on the property.

But here's the unforeseen bump in the road. To the new agent's surprise, the buyer isn't interested in the property anymore.

"No offers" speaks right to the heart of one of the most frustrating aspects of human nature: we don't trust ourselves. If your buyer is interested in a house that no one else wants, he can't help but think, "What did I miss?"

ɔo common to wonder why no one else wants what

Unfortunately, what happens then is that your client decides that he might not really want the house, either. He begins to look at the property in an entirely different light. *Now* he sees the power lines a block over. *Now* he *can* hear the freeway in the distance. It almost seems loud. He wonders what it will be like at night. Or the swimming pool — once his very favorite thing about the house — it doesn't seem big enough anymore. It not only looks outdated, but with those trees at the far end of the yard, the whole thing looks like one big cleaning headache!

No other bids on a property? One thing is pretty certain: your client is going to see that house in a negative light and is going to immediately feel like he or she needs more time to consider.

Now, a sharp agent will dig and find out that there has just been a *substantial* price reduction on the house and that his buyers are the first ones to see it. Or maybe it just fell out of escrow because the previous buyers couldn't obtain a loan. Or maybe the house just hit the market and your buyer is the very first one to get a tour.

You need to know these things and be able to quickly pass them on to your client.

Good agents ask questions. If I find there are no offers on a house that my clients love, I don't hang up and run to tell my client. Instead, I immediately ask the listing agent, "I'll bet you're expecting multiple offers on this house by the end of the weekend, right?"

Of course the listing agent usually answers in the affirmative. *That's* human nature, too.

When I find out that multiple offers are expected, then it's *me* who makes the call. I call my client and tell them what I've been told: that the listing agent is expecting multiple offers by Sunday night.

Then I tell my client that we better move fast!

Now the buyer suddenly develops another classic human response, which I call the "fear of loss." The "fear of loss" is a far more powerful fear than *not* wanting to buy something that no one else wants, because everyone wants to buy what they are about to lose (or what they are told they can't have). The sense of urgency that comes over us when we believe we'll *never* find another house *exactly* like the one we are poised to lose is a pretty powerful motivator.

I then urge my buyer to make an offer *right away* to avoid a bidding war, which is actually sort of funny. It's funny because I actually love bidding wars.

Why Bidding Wars Are Great!

I'm *very* comfortable in multiple-offer situations. I not *only* see them as both exciting and manageable, I incorporate them into my strategy as an important part of negotiation. A part that I'm going to utilize to get my client their dream house!

I admit that it wasn't always that way. When I first started out in real estate, one of the hardest calls I had to make was to listing agents to see if there were any offers on a house that my client wanted. When the listing agent would casually say, "Yeah, there's six offers already," it was like being socked in the stomach! All my work was down the drain. Only one of seven offers? How are we going to stand out against that!? The match wasn't even over yet, but I would feel defeated. Depression would actually set in!

Depression would set in, that is, just before panic. My job, I thought, had *suddenly* gotten harder. Multiple offers? My head would start to spin. I would think, "If I don't win, I'm going to lose." My mind would race. What if the *next* house my client wants also has multiple offers? What if we *never* find a house? What if every house has multiple offers for the rest of my career?

Thankfully, it didn't take me very long to learn that multiple offers were a *very good thing*. Because after a few go-rounds with clients who got cold feet right after finding out that *no one else* wanted their dream property — with more than a few drastic changes of heart *painfully* late in the process — I began to notice that the multiple-offer situations that I had won for my clients resulted in virtually *no* instances of cold feet.

Go Big or Go Home!

It's pretty simple: a multiple-offer situation confirms to your clients that they have truly found the right house. When you go into battle with your client *and win*, that house looks better than ever. *Everybody loves* what they are about to lose. Everyone *wants* what they can't have. Yet, everyone also loves what they have to fight for. Because getting something you had to fight for or something you had to work for by winning hard-fought battles is much, *much* sweeter than winning blowouts or, worse, winning when no one else shows up.

And that's okay. We're in real estate and part of our job is to help people win in the battle for their dream homes. We *have* to be good.

It's also a fact of our business that multiple-offer situations are inevitable. They are going to happen. And the truth is that I know *exactly* what to do to win whenever I'm involved in a multiple-offer situation. The truth is that I actually do love them! *I thrive on them!*

I've never actually done the numbers, but I would estimate that I've won in multiple-offer situations 90% of the time. *Ninety percent!* Because this is competition and it's *exactly* like sports in that preparation is *everything!* And if you go into multiple-offer situations prepared with a winning strategy that gives you an edge, you can outwit your opponents and score victory after victory for your clients and for your family.

Let's start at the beginning of the process. You are out showing a client various properties. You pull up to a house and right away they get excited. It hits them *just right.* They begin to point out the things about the property that they already love. You might even notice they start to hold hands or clutch one another's arm. Good signs. They whisper to one another because choosing a house is one of the most emotional decisions a person can make and they are seeing the possibility of their lives unfolding on that very spot.

I love that feeling. When *they* get excited, *I* get excited!

Once you get inside the house their affection for the property only grows. The family room. The kitchen. The upgrades. The extra bedroom. The backyard. The large shower. The angle of the lot. This is it! This is the house of their dreams! They love it!

And now you have to get it for them.

That sensation you feel in the pit of your stomach is the fear that you will call the listing agent and he'll already have multiple offers on the table. We've all felt it. I used to feel it. Maybe you *still* feel it every time this happens.

Would you like to be free of that feeling *forever?*

But first things first. Your clients love the house and now you must call the listing agent.

If I call and the listing agent says to me, "There are no offers on this property," then I immediately ask, "Are you expecting any?" Or I ask, "But you *are* expecting some soon, right?"

Oftentimes, an agent that is expecting an offer is the best scenario of all. An agent who is expecting an offer (or two) creates for your client almost the same sense of urgency as if there were *already* offers on the table.

No offers . . . yet. But the listing agent says that some are coming? I phone my clients and tell them that an offer(s) is coming, and if they hurry, they can avoid a bidding war.

But what about when the listing agent boasts an offer? Or even *several* offers? What then?

The ABCs of Winning Multiple Offers

The first thing that I do when a listing agent tells me that he has multiple offers on a house is to congratulate him. He's found a great house, a house that other people want.

Yet it also happens to be a house that *my* client wants. And *that* is when the competition begins. And *that* is when we earn our money. *That* is when the good and the great in our industry stand apart. The cream now has a chance to rise to the top!

How many offers are too many? There is absolutely no number you should fear. In the world of REOS, 35 offers are not uncommon. So follow this strategy and *expect* to win the majority.

I know a lot of realtors whose *only* strategy for winning in multiple-offer situations is to throw a lot of money at the seller. They get on the elevator and go up and up and up and keep pushing buttons until they get to the top floor.

That's foolish.

Multiple offers? Here's what I do: Because it's all about terms I begin with my client. I tell my client that we are going to put terms into the offer that will cost *them* nothing, but which will mean *everything* to the listing agent and to the seller.

I ask my buyer what he wants to offer for the house. The house is listed at $300,000 and there are already multiple offers on the table (we don't know for how much). They want the house. Their competitive juices are flowing. They may offer full price, or even higher. They may offer only $280,000.

Here is where I go to work. *Here* is where I introduce "special terms," each of which is a vital cog in a larger process of getting us that house. First, when the competition is going to close in 30 or 45 days, we are going to offer to close in just 10 days. I have devoted an entire chapter of *Momentum* to the power of the 10-day close because I believe it's one of the most powerful weapons in all of real estate. The reasons are obvious: the listing agent gets a paycheck and the seller gets his proceeds. *All faster!* This is *but one* of the weapons in your arsenal, and make no mistake, to *consistently* win in multiple-offer situations, you are going to need them all.

Back to terms: you put in the contract that you are willing to close in 10 days, but you are *actually* going to allow the seller to stay put for up to 30 days past COE. That's right! The seller simply makes the PITI payment to your buyer — just as they would *normally* make that payment to the bank — for however long they need to remain in the house, up to 30 days.

The seller can stay for up to 30 days because your ultimate goal is to get the house. Closing in 10 days automatically gets the listing agent on your side, while at the same time, allowing the seller to stay in the property after close of escrow *automatically* gets the *seller* listening to you — even though you have potentially offered less than *anyone else* bidding on the property.

Remember, the listing agent wants to get paid in 10 days, *not 30 or 45*. The seller wants the deal done fast so he can pay bills, pack up his belongings in peace, and start to sleep again. So now both the seller *and* the listing agent are looking in *your direction* over the heads of the competition. Already those 20 or 30 *other* offers are starting to sound like white noise in the background as they wade through the crowd toward *you*.

> The seller can stay for up to 30 days because your ultimate goal is to get the house.

But a simple 10-day close is only the beginning. You're going to need more, especially when others are driving the price up because they have nothing else to offer. *Their* only answer to beating the competition is to throw more money at the seller. Wow.

The second weapon at your disposal concerns the deposit. Everyone else is putting up about 1%, or a $3,000 deposit on a $300,000 house. Some buyers say, "I only want to put up $2,000, I don't want to risk a lot."

But here's where our 10-day close again works in our favor: I recommend you actually *double* the pot and put down $6,000.

Think about it: 3.5% down of $300,000 is $11,500. You eventually have to bring in over $11,000 anyway, so why not bring *more* up-front? Why not just bring $6,000 into the deposit up-front? Here's how the seller sees it: I tell him, we've got $6,000 reasons to close escrow — compared to $3,000. In other words, I ask them, "If this deal falls apart" (which we protect ourselves against each and every step of the way) "would you rather have $6,000 or $3,000?"

This makes the listing agent feel even more secure at the same time it gets us the *seller's* full attention. Now *the seller* is in our corner with the listing agent, and all the other standard offers don't look so exciting.

But we aren't even close to finished.

The third irresistible component of our unique terms revolves around the loan contingency. We're talking about buyers with multiple years at the same job and high FICO scores. These are people who are *extremely* qualified, so there's no problem. With these types of well-qualified clients, we don't have a loan contingency because we don't need it. The competition usually leaves their loan contingency intact, but I recommend doing that only if your client is shaky in terms of qualifying.

The second part of leaving off the loan contingency is, let's just suppose that there *is* a problem. If the competition removes their contingencies, and if they can't close in 30 days, *they lose their deposit*, which is why they *only* want to put up a $2,000 deposit to begin with. The difference for us is that, *because* we are closing so fast, we are *contingent the entire time*, so our buyer's $6,000 is *never at risk*. (As for the 17-day appraisal contingency, we used to get rid of it. But these days, with review appraisal, it's dangerous to be without, so I *strongly* recommend you leave it in if you are doing a 30-day COE.)

The next thing you must do to win in a multiple-offer situation also revolves around changing the way sales happen. Just about everyone else allows 17 days to do a home inspection, 17 days for due diligence. Everyone else allows 17 days for no other reason than "*that's* the way it's always been done."

Not anymore.

I recommend cutting this down to *seven days*. If you are the seller and you were going to have to wait a full 17 days to find out if your deal is solid, and now you have a buyer with terms that say "I will commit in seven days!" just who would you choose: the offer with the seven-day terms, or the offer with the 17-day terms? Get on the phone. Call two or three inspectors if you have to. Someone can *easily* get there in the next three to five days.

Some of you might be thinking, "But you said your client was *always* contingent, yet your offer says you will complete all inspections and due diligence within seven days."

That's right! Because we are making appointments to sign loan documents on day #7, the seller and the listing agent never issue a 24-hour "notice to perform." The buyers never remove the inspection contingencies, and because we never actually remove the contingencies, we are *fully* contingent and can cancel at any time AND

> **Because we are closing so fast we are contingent the entire time.**

according to the California Purchase Agreement (and in every other state that I've seen) we get our full earnest-money deposit *back!*

But let's say they do actually issue a 24-hour notice to perform? Your buyer *still* doesn't have to comply. The *only* power the seller has in California is to cancel the sale and return the deposit to the buyer! End of story! With just 72 hours to the finish line, does anyone think they are going to cancel the sale and start the whole thing over? The fact is, while it's possible, that has never happened to me *ever!* Not once. They are always going to give it two or three days or a week, no problem. And if you are thinking, "I don't know if my lender can go that fast," there's a whole lot of information coming up in *Momentum* that deals *directly* with that exact facet of building your pipeline. But I can sum it up for you right now: if you don't know if your lender can move that fast then get a new lender! Plenty of lenders will move that fast and it's up to you to find them and work *only* with them. As part of the remake of your business, you need to find a "get it done" lender. If your lender whines that you are pushing them too hard, then you have a choice: stick with a whiner, or get yourself a go-to finisher! My bet is that once you show them that you're not going to be doing business as usual anymore, the good lenders, the *hungry, aggressive* lenders, will be knocking down your door! Just interview three to seven highly recommended lenders and you'll absolutely find a couple of reliable movers and shakers who have no problem working this fast.

One of the main messages of *Momentum* is learning how to create something that is next to impossible to stop. Something fast. Something recession-proof. Where the competition is trying to catch up to you! Where every deal is completed so quickly and so clean, it turns to gold! That's *momentum!*

So, who is the seller going to choose? Does he want to wait 17 days with someone else when he can deal with you and wait only seven days to find out if he or she has a solid deal? There's no mystery about who they are going to sell to. Who would *you* pick?

It's not even close. And you are giving the seller one more reason to choose you even though your buyer has offered *less* than everyone else (we'll get to that in a moment). You are giving the seller a larger earnest-money deposit, $6,000 over $3,000. You're offering a quicker close of escrow: 10 days versus 30. No loan contingency. Due diligence in seven days instead of 17. You are yelling, "Pick us! Pick us! Pick us!" and I guarantee you the seller is listening loud and clear. He will pick you, there's no risk, and it's not going to cost you or your buyer an extra *anything*.

Moving Too Fast to Wait for Reports

The next way you are going to get your client the house of their dreams in multiple-offer situations relates to the pest report. Everyone asks for one. Everyone has *always* asked for one. *Everyone*, that is, *except you.*

That's right. *You are no longer going to ask for a pest report.*

The seller's agent is going to see that you didn't request a report — and if he doesn't see it YOU are going to point it out to him — and then he is going to point it out to his client.

Now, the seller is already extremely worried that he might have some monster expenses. He's going to have 15 offers on the table and yours has the fastest and easiest terms and you aren't even asking them to do a pest report or clearance.

Negotiate that later! Why negotiate a clearance *before* you even know if you need one or not?

Don't worry, this is perfectly safe *and* it's going to get your client the house. You aren't going to let anyone buy a house that hasn't been inspected. Because during your due diligence — *after* you've already won the multiple-offer situation — you are going to order a pest report and have your buyer pay for it. This way, you'll not *only* know if there are any hidden problems, but if you find any you can cancel the sale and get your deposit money back. Remember, any other agent would have thought he or she was *protecting* their client by having a pest report as part of the terms. You leave it out for now, where its absence becomes an asset.

> **You are no longer going to ask for a pest report.**

The next wrinkle in the special terms that I offer actually cracks me up! Unless it's an REO, virtually *no one* buys homes "as is." No one writes "as is" in big letters on the contract because those words scare the heck out of people.

Naturally, the concern is ... what if something *is* wrong

with the roof or the air conditioner? I've seen three-year-old air conditioners that cost $7,000 and were *completely* worthless. So what if something *is* wrong?

I cannot emphasize this enough: what you want, what you are aiming for, what *Momentum* is *mostly* about, is gaining control of the decision-making process for you and your buyer. *You* want the house offered to you and your buyer so that you can make the decision about whether to carry the deal through. Just because you agree to buy the house "as is" doesn't mean that you *can't* conduct your due diligence. *Of course you can!*

So, in the course of your due diligence you find out that the roof is bad? You're not going to fork over $14,000 for a new roof. So if during your client's due diligence you find a problem, you go to the seller and tell them, "I'm sorry, but during the due diligence we found you have a serious problem with your roof. We're going to have to cancel the sale."

I guarantee you that the seller's agent will call you and say, "If we put on a new roof" (or repair the problem) "will you stay with the deal?"

Of course we'll stay with the deal! Was it my intention to get a new roof? *Absolutely not!* I hope the roof and air conditioner are perfect. But no one is going to buy a house with a bad roof, or a defective air conditioner, or termites, et cetera.

Whereas just a few days before you were lumped in with a crowd of 15 or 20 other buyers — all your hands raised asking the seller to pick you — *now* you are standing in front of the class getting a gold medal because the seller just chose your offer! It's congratulations time! You won again!

How do you stand out? How do you get the sale when everyone is screaming to be chosen? Your terms and your machine *have* to be squeaky clean and fine-tuned. They *must* be irresistible to both the seller and the seller's agent, and "as is" is just one more irresistible reason to pick us.

Closing the Deal

I was coaching a group of agents recently, and I asked them if they ever have their lender call the listing agent and brag about their client. None of them said yes, but having my lender call is something I always do. It's the fourth quarter of the big game and with the terms I've outlined you are ahead by three touchdowns. The game *should* be over, but you don't want to quit just yet, because the game is *not* over until your client is chosen and the deal is done.

So the very last thing I do to seal the deal is have my lender call the listing agent and brag about my client. Not just an approval letter or an email, but an actual phone call. I tell the listing agent that my lender will be calling him in five minutes and that he wants to answer any questions they may have about my buyer. So all the other normal, old-fashioned, typical offers have a 30-day close, a $3,000 deposit, a 17-day loan contingency, a 17-day appraisal contingency, a 17-day inspection contingency, a request for a pest report, a request for a clear Section 1, and no thought of writing "as is" in the contract. They don't do this because typical buyers want the right to *ask* for repairs.

Now, contrast those terms with a 10-day (or an eight-day) close, a $6,000 deposit, no loan contingency, a 17-day appraisal contingency (remember, we leave that in due to review appraisals), a seven-day inspection contingency, no pest report, no clear Section 1, the emphasis that we'll take the home "as is" AND we have our lender call and brag about the client, and YOU will get the house almost every time.

Typically, the listing agent comes back to me and says, "We love your terms, but you are outgunned by $50,000." I expect this (though it doesn't always happen). So what is my reply? Simple: "Give me a counteroffer."

Remember, the listing agent is on your side. You are the one paid in 10 days. Just get a counteroffer. If they love ut want the offer sweetened a little, then great! We are getting that house. And if we decide not to raise the offer, it's *our choice.*

When you write smart, strategic offers like this, offers that cost your buyer nothing but actually appeal to the listing agent *and* the seller, then if there's some price negotiation upwards, it still leaves you and your client solidly in the driver's seat.

Another HUGE benefit of winning in multiple-offer situations is that when you get your client a house over 17 other offers, then your client thinks you are the greatest agent in the world (and maybe you are). Not only will they be your clients for life, but their good word of mouth will bring you droves of other clients.

Many of you know *exactly* what if feels like to get beaten house after house after house. It's a terrible feeling and it demoralizes you *and* your client. No one wants to lose even one time, let alone half a dozen times (or even more). Losses like that, even if it's not entirely your fault, will soon get your client wondering if perhaps the problem isn't *you!*

So remember that there is *absolutely* a way to win in multiple-offer situations. While most agents have no better strategy than to throw money at the seller, you have something better. You don't need to waste your client's money in a bidding war to get them a house that 10 or even 20 other buyers are fighting for.

Remember, a traditional offer promises:

- 30-day close
- $3,000 earnest-money deposit
- 17-day loan contingency
- 17-day inspection contingency
- 17-day appraisal contingency
- The right to ask for repairs
- The seller to provide a pest report
- A clear Section 1
- A prequalification letter or a pre-approval letter

All this does is get your client in a bidding war and wastes thousands of dollars.

By comparison, a strategic, smart offer has this:

- A 10-day close
- $6,000 earnest-money deposit
- No loan contingency
- 7-day inspection contingency
- No appraisal contingency (ONLY WHEN YOU ARE 100% SURE OF VALUE)
- Your buyer offering to buy the house "as is"
- No pest report requested
- No Section 1 requested
- Pre-approval letter with a call from the lender

Using smart, strategic offers, I win in multiple-offer situations a majority of the time. My clients *routinely* get houses where there are 10 or more bids, and where they are outbid by thousands, if not tens of thousands, of dollars. I would put my method of strategic offers up against ANY other method *anywhere* and feel *extremely* confident that my buyer will get their dream house. And by incorporating these terms into your business, you can separate yourself from the herd and become the *go-to* agent in your town.

FOUR
FOUR
FOUR

The Power of the 10-Day Close

I've been fortunate enough to speak to hundreds of groups of people who work in real estate. That's thousands of individuals from every region of the country. Each time I speak the first thing I usually ask is, "How long is your typical escrow period?"

Almost without fail the answer is 30 days.

Whenever I hear 30 days, my next question is always, "Why does it take you 30 days to close?"

Some people stare blankly back at me. Some agents get a little defensive. Others give me a shrug, then say things like, "That's just the way it is." They look at me like I've just asked them why the sky is blue, or why the grass is green.

Thirty-day closes, it seems, are just the way it is.

Sunrise, sunset.

Thirty days. *Thirty days.* THIRTY DAYS! You'd think I'd be used to hearing it by now, but that response still both frustrates and amazes me. I have to admit that when agents respond "Thirty days" it actually makes *me* just a little bit defensive.

Let's say you are new to real estate and you want to start out right. Or let's say you've been in the game a while, you work hard and have built a solid reputation, but you *just can't seem* to get over that hump. The sales are trickling in and you wonder,

"How can I make more?" You have a long list of clients and a good referral tree. You're doing something right. Maybe you even have a team. But there are only so many hours in a day. You take one step forward but it's followed by one step back. Year after year after year, each and every deal just seems to drag on and on and on and on.

Have you ever thought to yourself, "If only I could make it all go *faster?*"

That's how I felt for several years. My income plateaued, and I just could not break through and make more. I had a couple more children, bought a bigger house, and what was once a great income began to seem like less and less.

I felt like I was going in reverse.

There are well over one million real estate agents in America. So, needless to say, you have to develop razor-sharp edges all over your business model. You have to be open-minded, proactive, and you have to find or even *create* ways to get those edges.

But how?

How? What? Why?

After a few years in real estate, and after over 100 sales — but just a few of those near-perfect, super-fast closes — it occurred to me that the fast ones felt so good, so enjoyable, and were so natural because FAST CLOSES were *exactly* the way it was all supposed to

> **The faster the deal the less that goes wrong.**

work in a perfect business world. It felt good to be in control. It felt good to make money fast.

About that time, something else pretty incredible occurred to me: I realized that *less* went wrong if the deal closed fast. That's right! *The faster the deal the less that goes wrong.* Plus, fast closes meant I had more time to work, play, and earn more money. Every time I closed a fast deal, the extra time I *used* to spend waiting on lenders and appraisers was then all mine to pursue more business.

Remember, learning how to get more — more sales and more money — out of the same amount of time is one of the primary goals of *Momentum*.

Because my first fast closes actually resulted in more opportunity and fewer problems, just like that I became determined to figure out how to make all my deals happen as fast as possible.

Ten days! That's 240 hours. That's 14,400 minutes. Regardless of the measurement, *whenever* we closed fast it took a well-oiled and highly-motivated collective effort to get it done.

But were those fast closes just flukes? At some point a light went off inside my head. I'd completed enough fast closes to know that there was *absolutely no* reason we couldn't do business like that *almost* every time.

I just had to get the other principals to think like I did.

The 10-day close is literally about the transformation of the real estate industry in the United States. It concerns the progression of technology. It concerns the speeding-up of our society and an altering of current perceptions and accepted real estate business norms. It involves tweaking your partners in business to think outside the box so that a transfer of control, powered by you, *back to you*, takes place. In short, the mastering of the 10-day close is the point in your professional life in which you stop waiting on everyone else and instead begin to help all those people involved in the transaction understand why it's to their advantage to close extremely fast.

The Way It's Always Been

When I need a little inspiration to remind me just how drastically things can change, I head to Starbucks. Look at what Starbucks did — not just to coffee — *but also to our society and our culture*. Starbucks didn't invent coffee. But they did *transform* the coffee industry. They did this by selling a 50-cent cup of coffee *and* making it a pleasant-enough experience that millions of us began to allot time each day for special trips to get some of their product. They gave us *fast*, multiple coffee choices.

When you think about it, it's pretty amazing: Starbucks reached into a society that was *already* complaining about not having enough time to get things done, and then made it a virtual necessity — and a chic, cool way to start every day — by convincing us to stop off at one of their shops. Starbucks didn't *just* change an industry ... they *created* one.

Real estate has had a few transformations and innovations. But the truth is that real estate really hasn't had its "Starbucks moment" in terms of creating an industry within an industry. The unfortunate truth is that we realtors seem content to do things the old-fashioned way. The way they've always been done.

But the old-fashioned way is unacceptable to me. We sell real estate to make money. And yet, despite many technological innovations, one of the only ways most realtors can come up with to make more money is to work harder. That's right. Get more listings and sell more homes. Never mind if a buyer or seller gets cold feet, or if you allow your clients to lead you on and on and on. You just have to persevere, and then you have to get more listings and sell more homes.

Working hard is the American way and I both subscribe to *and* endorse it. So as long as you make time for your family, your health, and your faith, good things just seem to happen for people who work hard.

But just working hard simply is not enough. It used to be, I'll grant you that, but not anymore. You are limited by the number of hours in a day. And, unless you train them correctly, you are also subject to the whims of fickle buyers and sellers.

But what other way is there?

You have to work *smarter*.

Momentum is packed with ways to maximize the time you spend selling real estate. And while I'm confident that these lessons will work for you, *the single best way that I've found to make more money* FASTER *in real estate takes nothing more than a shifting of the focus on who directs and controls the transaction.* A shifting of the focus away from the old-fashioned scheduling of the other interested principals — the lenders, the appraisers, the agents — back a full 180 degrees towards you.

> The single best way to make more money faster in real estate takes nothing more than a shifting of the focus on who directs and controls the transaction.

Think about an action movie where the heat-seeking missile misses its target, only then to turn around in midair and home back in for the strike. That missile is business and opportunity, and that's how you want business to be directed: right back at you so that you have control. This complete redirection will result in one of two things happening, and both are wonderful: either you'll make more money faster, or you'll have more free time.

How Do I Make the Shift?

To perfect the 10-day close you have to be willing to change your thinking a little. All the reasons that it traditionally took 30 days to close escrow are no longer true today. It used to take a couple of weeks to get an appraisal. It used to take a couple of weeks to get a home inspection.

But with the improvement of technology, specifically the Internet, everything we believed about the timelines of business communication was rendered obsolete. Now you can have contracts printed and signed and loans approved in a matter of hours. Regarding the duration of closes, the fact is that you can wake up tomorrow having forgotten that there's *ever* been any standard time for them.

So put on those "first-time eyes" one more time. And get ready to feel completely free and justified in throwing whatever you know about closings out the window, because you are about to begin again.

The 10-Day Close Begins with Sellers — Scratch Them Where They Itch

Earlier, I spoke about the other interested principals of real estate. If you want to close most deals in 10 days, start with the seller. If you want to please a seller and get them to work with you, you've got to first give them what they want. And we all know what they want, don't we? Money. Cash in hand. Freedom. No stress. Smooth transactions.

Here's an example: your client is trying to buy a $400,000 home and the seller still owes $200,000. If you're willing to close escrow in 10 days — with very few exceptions — you are giving the seller *exactly* what he wants, and it won't matter if there are 10 other offers on the table. Ninety percent of the time you and your client will be the seller's choice.

Here's why: Giving a seller what he wants gives you bargaining power. You are satisfying them by giving them quick, painless money that gets them out from under the financial obligation of their house *fast*. The listing agent wants to get paid as well. Would you like to wait 30 days to get paid when you could get paid in 10 days? The seller gets his proceeds fast. The listing agent gets paid fast.

You Had Me at "Hello"

Many people are struggling. Many people are extremely cash-poor. What this means to you is that sellers are more motivated and more flexible than at any time in the recent past. You can buy a three-bedroom home, in most states anyway, for a mere $90,000. That's rolling the clock back more than a decade. That's value. Media hype aside, a vast majority of homeowners are still making their payments *on time*. Yes, this economy has added stress and it takes every bit of our wits and ingenuity to get by. But honestly? The sky is not falling down on everyone. And things will improve. However, the coming boom may not be the unbelievable price escalation *and* demand that we've all recently enjoyed. Instead, the coming boom will probably be almost entirely value-based. Value, which means that your clients can afford to buy a terrific home in a decent neighborhood for less money than at any time since 1998.

The 10-day close is a great tool in a good economy. But in a tough economy? It's your best friend. Your secret weapon. Your ace in the hole. Because I know real estate agents who are enjoying boom-times right this minute. We are in the "buy low" of a classic buy low-sell high cycle. Bank repos and short sales are introducing a boom, and lots of people are doing very well financially by positioning themselves for the up cycle that will invariably come again. And having a fast close in your pocket gives you the edge.

The Sacramento-area economy is one of the worst in America. But right now, five or even 10 offers on a bank repo are pretty typical. This means that there's a lot of competition for every sale. So, whether it's a bank repo or just a desirable property, if I'm trying to secure a house for a client and there are 10 offers on the table, what are my odds of getting the sale?

My odds are excellent! In fact, more often than not it's *my* buyer who wins and gets the house. It's *my* buyer who walks away with the property. My buyers win these battles because I'm ready to wage war with a 10-day close that will deliver a paycheck to the listing agent, and cash to the seller, *three weeks faster than the competition.* So even if we get beat on the price (which we usually do), the seller comes back to us to negotiate because we have an ace up our sleeve: and that ace is the fast money and easy terms of the 10-day close. (I'll repeat this again later, but remember to always coach the listing agent to come back to you with a counteroffer.)

Because *That's* Just the Way It's Always Been

When I tell people about the 10-day close, most follow along and get very excited. Eventually, however, I see the lightbulb go off above their head. The old way of thinking creeps in and their excitement wanes and they look down. It's at this moment that I can tell he or she is thinking, "What if the property is still occupied?" (which it usually is) "Where is the seller going to go after 10 days?"

This answer may surprise you, but the seller isn't going to go anywhere at all.

When we close in 10 days instead of 30, I encourage the buyer to let the seller stay the entire 30 days (or even 60 days if need be).

Here's how: first, the most important facet, the business spigot — the money faucet, if you will — of the 10-day close is that we are giving the seller what he wants and needs: money and a fast out. If you give the seller money in 10 days, and then let them stay put another 20, you are relieving them of their stress, their worries, their problems! You are putting an end to their anxieties *right now!* And, frankly, putting an end to the fears of the seller is one of the very best tools in real estate today.

But 10 days? 20 days? 30 days? Who cares? *Everyone does.* First, cash is king. You pay someone in 10 days, and right off the top you will see a *maximum* price reduction. The ease. The stress relief. Most sellers owe money on both their homes *and* their credit cards, so a fast close, plus fast money, equals an amenable seller.

Here are some examples: I've seen sellers of $1.5 million homes drop the asking price $100,000 down to $1.4 million just because of the 10-day close. I've seen sellers who previously would not budge — I mean *would not budge* even *one dollar* in their asking price — many, *many* times I've seen these same sellers drop the price $50,000 because of the appeal of the 10-day close. The reason is simple: if you give the homeowner what he *really* wants, what he needs, you offer to get them out from under the rock both painlessly *and fast*, and 99% of the time they will *substantially* lower their price.

Yes, closing fast is that important. But as you'll soon see, it's not all just about cash.

Who's Against the 10-Day Close?

You know who is generally *against* the 10-day close? Lenders.
Lenders are taught to have pipelines. They're taught that if they
are going to be successful they need to have 10, 20, 30, 40 loans
in their pipeline, which is a nice way of saying "in their pocket."
Ten days to close? It threatens to mess up their manufacturing-
plant assembly line — which is outside their comfort zone,
because it scrambles the duration of their loan cycles. Lenders
are very comfortable controlling a system that requires you and
me to jump through their hoops.

But here's how I see it: it's the real estate agents that typically
give lenders the business, so why shouldn't we dictate the pace?
I say: *if your lender can't move fast enough to consistently close in
10 days, get a new lender!* Interview and find people who can get
the job done. Rock and roll! Slay some dragons! Get it done
now! No more excuses!

Financially, lenders don't see an advantage to closing quickly.
But why? Sure, they'd get paid faster, but they have been the
engine of real estate commerce for so long, they've grown ac-
customed to dictating the speed of the transaction.

Plus, lots of people are begging certain lenders for money.

Well, I have just one thing to say about that: We're not going
to let lenders dictate the speed of the close anymore. So if the
lender says to you, "I don't know if I can get an appraisal in the
next four or five days," then it's time for you to find a lender
who has a *can-do, agent-friendly* attitude!

Appraisal in five days? No problem! Close escrow in 10 days?
I'm on it! The 110% hustle is the name of the game. Focused.
Results-driven.

I find letting lenders control the speed of the real estate transaction unacceptable, and so should you. So here's how I light
a fire underneath a lender: if a lender won't work with me to
make a 10-day close happen, with only rare exceptions, I won't

work with them again, and I tell them so right from the start. Because there is no legal or logical reason to drag closings out over 30 days, I won't do it. I want to get paid, and I want to win in multiple-offer situations. This requires a 10-day close. The lenders I work with understand this. It didn't happen overnight, but I found and I work with people who are motivated and versed in 10-day closings. So if you are in an established market with an antiquated, old-school, hierarchical way of doing things, then switch your business to find the motivated, hungrier lenders and grow with them. *My* pipeline starts with hungry lenders who are flexible and willing to work with *Brent Gove Intensity.* I like working that way and I make more money because of it.

How do you pick a good lender? Start with three to five referrals, interview them, and find a good personality fit for you. They don't all have to be hyperactive workaholics, they just have to be driven, sincere, reliable and honest. That's all there is to it! But how do you know? Because you can't read minds, I suggest old-fashioned trial and error. After a positive referral and an acceptable interview, if you still have a good feel for them and they have a good reputation, then the next thing I do is to throw them some juicy bones in the form of loans. If they are competent, and your feedback from your clients is positive — if they have a good bedside manner and treat your clients with respect — then get the job done! Their word, like your word, is their bond. If they're late on something — especially in the beginning of the partnership — then just make certain it's only a day or two *at most.*

There are, of course, other things you must look for if you are going to build a long-term business relationship. For instance, if your lender makes a mistake, do they admit it? Do they own up to it? Do they do everything in their power to make it right? The interest rate must be what they quoted. The closing costs must be what they quoted. Are they working hard to grow and be well-connected? Do they have a database and actually use it?

Because this relationship is a two-way street. You want to utilize them, and you want them to utilize you. You are sending clients their way and you should expect them to reciprocate. What this means is that when someone with *manageable credit* comes to them for a loan, remind them that you would like them to be referred to *you*.

How Does a 10-Day Close Increase Your Income?

How does the 10-day close increase your income? First, a 10-day close will free you up to pursue other leads and other sales. That may sound simple, but it *cannot* be overstated. You are finding creases and space in your already packed schedule by streamlining the transaction process. And the following is huge: when the friends, family, and neighbors of the people you just helped close escrow in 10 days ask them, "How did you close so fast?" the arrow will be pointing right at you. Of all the many components to building a successful franchise, referrals are one of the most important and *lucrative* facets of your pipeline.

Second: you'll make more money with the 10-day close because when a seller has to mull over multiple offers with typical 30–45 day closes, and your client offers the seller a 10-day close, the seller will go with your client *95% of the time*. The seller will choose you and your client, even when you are outbid, because the allure of the 10-day sale is so appealing that even if you are drastically outbid, before making a final decision, out of common sense, the seller will almost *always* come to you first and ask you to raise your offer. This puts you in control and gives you the opportunity to ask them for a counter. This gives you options. You can raise your price. You can sell them on the benefits of your fast close. Or you can simply choose to walk away. But my experience is that they won't let you walk very far. You are in control. *You* are in the driver's seat! The seller wants his proceeds. The listing agent wants his commission. They can have them in 30–45 days, *maybe*, or they can have them in 10. Who do you think gets the nod?

Don't forget that once you master the 10-day close, from that moment onward you have an ally on the selling side: the listing agent. The listing agent will *always* be your ally with fast closes. After all, do listing agents want 30 days of questions posed by the buyers, or would they prefer 10? Do listing agents want to wait 30 days to get paid, or would they prefer to get paid in 10? Which brings us to the third way the 10-day close increases your income: because *you* and your client get the house! The longer a deal is in the pipeline, the more that *can* go wrong. Acts of God, wars, job losses, market crashes, cold feet — selling agents know this. And because they know this, you have an ally on the selling side of the aisle.

Dragging sales out over a month is just not good business for you, the realtor. What we are trying to do is give proceeds to the seller as fast as possible. Never forget that. Getting proceeds to the seller as fast as possible is the floodgate of the transaction. And while nothing happens without that gate opening, conversely, *everything* happens once you get that gate code. So why would you *ever* waste an entire month on one deal when you don't have to?

Can It Really All Get Done in 10 Days?

I'm constantly asked if escrows can consistently be closed in 10 days. And my answer is constantly the same: Absolutely! It's how I do business. I've wrapped complete deals in five days, and so can you. I've closed escrow in three days AND saved my buyer $50,000 in the process. I'm not talking about killing yourself here, or going at breakneck speed, because it's the exact same amount of work — just more concentrated and organized. But how do you make the 10-day close your bread and butter? First, you'll need to restructure parts of *your* pipeline — which doesn't always happen overnight. Trial and error and weeding out those people who aren't up to 10-day closings may take a few go-rounds, but it won't take long, and you may just be surprised at how agreeable even your existing contacts are. Go to them and ask them about the fastest closes they've handled. Gauge their interest in speeding up. If the answers aren't promising, you may need to approach a new lender and query them. And that's just fine! The important thing is that you are going to do it. It's a decision you need to make. You simply have to utilize your team, your assistant (if you have one), and your experience to get things done faster. In the end, you are reading this book to make more money. The 10-day close is one important tool because, first, you can begin today. Second, it won't take any additional training or money. And third, any savvy realtor can do it!

Another important facet of making the 10-day close your go-to method of doing business is not to mismanage expectations by begging loan officers to "help me close fast *this time*." If they think you're asking for a 10-day close just this once, you'll meet more resistance next time and have to change more members of your pipeline *more often*. I understand wanting something so bad you can taste it. But don't cut corners. You are starting anew and you are not just a one-trick pony. I realize that sometimes buyers have credit hang-ups and those circumstances require a longer close. That's fine! But don't beg or coerce your lender, because you absolutely want the 10-day close this deal, the next deal, and the next. You want the 10-day close almost every time! So don't ask for a favor from your loan officer as though it's just this once, because it most certainly is not. Starting today, you're changing the way you do business. You're re-writing the rules, just like Starbucks did with coffee and Google did with the Internet search engine. You don't say, "Let's go to Starbucks Coffee" or "Let's search the World Wide Web." The 10-day close is now your brand. It's your Band-Aid. Your Coca Cola. Your Jell-O. Your Kleenex. Shake it up! Don't plead. Be the 10-day close brand. Lead the way, and if you find resistance, no problem; politely find a new, more motivated crew, and take a different path that leads you to consistent 10-day closes, because they work, and because they help you! Ten-day closes help you *dramatically* negotiate lower prices for your buyers, and they give you an incredible edge that helps you win when competing in multiple-offer situations.

I'm going to go back to the beginning of my career. I hate to admit it, but I used to actually fear multiple offers. I honestly did. I didn't like to lose. I was competitive and I hated the idea of not having an edge. Multiple offers? It felt like chaos.

I'm thinking back to those times, and I'm smiling as I write this. I'm smiling because now I *absolutely* love multiple offers. I don't dread or fear them at all. Here's a side note: You ever notice that, when faced with multiple offers and competition, how often your client wants that house *even more* because that competitive charge goes off inside their head? We're Americans, and even when we say we aren't competitive, we still don't ever like to lose.

But besides having four aces in your hand in the form of a 10-day close, when it comes to satisfying your buyer, multiple offers can actually assist you. Simply, in what can be a stressful situation, multiple offers reaffirm your client's decision about having made an offer: everyone wants that house! *Remind* them of that. All the other buyers thought it was a great property for the money! Reaffirm their positive feelings about their judgments and impulses and desires. They made the right decision!

So they were smart to want that house. Everyone else wants it, too. And now they want to win. Now they want that house more than ever before.

And that's great for you!

Conversely, when there are no other offers, naturally, buyers wonder if they are making the right choice. And that fear and insecurity makes them react defensively. They demand more of you, and they demand more of the seller. But you have to remember why the buyer came to you: he or she needs an expert and this is a huge decision.

Let's face facts about human nature: it's difficult to accept that someone else knows more than you do. Want an example most of us can relate to? How about your last trip to the auto mechanic? The guy comes out of the garage with an invoice listing 300 car parts in a foreign language, and he has a list of charges for billable hours that you suspect stretches back to before you even owned the car. You don't know what those parts are. You don't know if that mechanic spent 72 hours under your hood.

But at some point you have to trust him. He's the expert. Look into his eyes. And when you drive your car off the lot and it drives like new? I have to admit that, right then, I usually think that whatever he charged me was worth it. It's worth it to have peace of mind. It's worth it to have an expert show me the way and to alleviate my fears about something that I have no idea about.

It makes me respect that auto mechanic because he is an expert.

And the best feeling in real estate? For me, it's coming through for my client and winning a contest with multiple offers. The truth is that we win more often than not, and we win because of the 10-day close. We win because the seller wants out and he chooses us because we can deliver money the fastest. We win because the seller comes back to *us* with the chance to counter, and while we *may not* raise our offer, the seller wants out and he chooses us. We win because we have control. We have our ducks in a row. We are offering something unique. We are serious buyers, and our ability to close in 10 days means we are serious bidders ready to make a deal. Finally, we win because we have an ally in the form of the seller's agent. He or she badly wants to turn the knob and open that floodgate of commerce, and the 10-day close is one gigantic motivator.

Set Real Deadlines — Closing the 10-Day Close

I used to be with RE/MAX. One particular year, out of over 10,000 agents, I qualified as the #2 agent in the state of California. As a reward for our success, RE/MAX took the top 250 elite agents on a cruise. During the cruise they asked me to teach a class, and so I agreed. Now, these were the most aggressive and successful agents in the state of California. So, of course, right away I asked the agents, "How long is an escrow?" They replied 30 days, 45 days, even 60 days. One person said 21 days. You know my opinion? Twenty-one days is twice what you need.

But that's why I believe that 10-day escrows will transform the industry. The agents that grab hold of them will be part of this historic change.

I don't win every bidding war. If there are 30 offers on the table, you might think your odds are 1 in 30. Occasionally, a listing agent will come back to me and say, "We love your terms, but are you willing to go to $585,000?"

When this happens I go to my clients and ask if they are willing to go that high. Sometimes the answer is yes, sometimes no. You can't win them all. But sometimes, surprisingly often, in fact, when we say no, the seller still comes back to us because of our terms and the 10-day close. The successful listing agents often go with us because they want to get the deal done. They appreciate that my buyer is organized. They like the idea of 10 days of questions rather than 30. After all, what if the rates shoot up in 30 days? The fact is, listing agents like the 10-day close so much that they often convince their client it's the best route as well. Plus I'm always there to remind them of the benefits.

So remember, the 10-day close offers you the following: Everyone gets paid sooner. The lender, the title company, the home appraisers, the seller, and you, *you,* you! And the buyer is the chosen one: the lucky recipient of the home.

Some people wonder, isn't a 10-day close dangerous? Let me tell you what's dangerous. Dangerous is a 30-day escrow. The contract says your loan appraisal and inspection contingencies are going to be removed in 17 days (in most states). In 17 days agents issue what is called a "24-hour notice to perform." A 24-hour notice to perform means you have to remove all your contingencies or the seller has the right to cancel the sale. So agents go to their clients and say, "The 17 days are up. The appraisal came in, it's good. The inspection is good. We reviewed the disclosures, everything's fine. It's time to remove the contingencies. Are you happy with everything?"

So the buyer removes their contingencies. But the problem is that this doesn't guarantee that the client is going to get a loan. I have seen people lose as much as $10,000 earnest money when their lender, who had said that the loan was rock solid, came back and said that the underwriter had rejected their time on the job. They didn't like that the buyer had gone from a forklift operator to an ambulance driver and had only been employed for a year. They want more experience, or they don't feel the level of employment is sufficient.

Now the loan has fallen through. To me, that's dangerous! Now the buyer is frantically trying to get a new loan. Now they are grabbing at the first available loan at 6% instead of 4.75%.

When you close in 10 days you are covered for the entire period: through the loan, the appraisal, and the inspection contingency. They are all in place and the buyer is safe. Of course, what if the listing agent tries to get your client to remove *all* contingencies in seven, eight, or nine days? My advice is the same thing you tell your teenagers: Just say no!

So, what's wrong with the old, antiquated way of doing business? If you want to risk your client's earnest-money deposit, your hard work, and the hard work of the other folks involved, you can. But when people ask if the 10-day close is safe, I say, why would you do business any other way? I mean it! It's the safest. It's the fastest. It's *professional, and it's efficient!*

How many times have you gotten the legwork done in five or seven days? The appraisal and the inspection and the loan are in place. Then what's next? Waiting 25 more days to close escrow?! It's madness! No thanks. And you know why you wait?

Because the lender has that pipeline. You are paying $5,000 to $10,000 more for that house, and that's for a $200,000 home.

The most common reason I get from agents as to why they don't do the 10-day close is that they don't think their lender will do them. My first question is, have you asked? And if you have asked and been turned down, then I have only one thing to say: get a new lender! Again, these are not just words on the page, I mean this. Let's be reasonable. *If your horse can't get around the track fast enough to win, you get a new horse.* You need some horsepower!

> **If your horse can't get around the track fast enough to win, you get a new horse.**

Here's a story that I love to tell: since the late 1500s the Swiss made the best timepieces in the world. For almost 500 years a tightly wound Swiss watch was considered the best watch anywhere.

But along came technology. The Swiss watchmakers were offered the technology for digital chips. One by one by one they all thumbed their noses at it. Now, 95% of the world's watches are made in Asia and the Swiss make less than 2%.

Now, deep down, do I wish that the Swiss still made all the world's watches in the shadow of the Alps? Sure I do. I like tradition. I like the idea of Swiss watches. But things change. And you have to be willing to embrace that change. Do not make the mistake of thumbing your noses at 10-day closes. Grow and evolve with the business climate. Be the first to master them and you will become the agent people come to for business and advice. You will be the leader. You will make more money and you will be the dominant agent in your marketplace!

The final component of perfecting 10-day closes revolves around the seller. If you're thinking that most sellers won't possibly be able to move out in 10 days, you're probably right. But it doesn't matter, because, if need be, you're going to give them an extra 30 days to move out. That's right! Tell them to simply take the mortgage payment that they would have made to the bank and instead make it payable directly to your buyer. If the seller owns the house outright, then come up with a reasonable rent.

I'm hardly a softy, but I'm fair. Depending on the circumstances, I usually have no problem giving away a month for free. It's important to remember that your goal was to get the house. *You* and your client have gotten the property, which was your main objective all along. You have succeeded. You have gotten a house over multiple offers. *Your goal isn't to move into the house in 10 days, it's to win the war!* So, really, do you want one month's rent, or do you want this fantastic house?

How often have you seen deals fall through because of the smallest details? Details equal delays. Be amenable when you have victory in hand. Ten-day closes eliminate tons of small details that can derail your deal. With cash in hand the seller is usually *extremely* relieved and more than happy to pay a month's mortgage or market rent right to your buyer. The greatest feeling in the world is to hand the keys to your buyer well *before* the rest of the buyers and agents bidding on the property know what hit them. They're regrouping and looking for other properties only to find you already waiting when they arrive, another 10-day close in hand.

> Your goal isn't to move into the house in 10 days, it's to win the war!

A 10-day close effectively turns your buyer into a cash buyer. The funny thing is that many cash buyers close in 30 days because they have an agent who is not thinking or not effectively looking out for their best interests (or their own).

Don't let that be you.

Momentum has an entire chapter on winning in multiple-offer situations. And while there are loads of lessons in that chapter that you can apply to winning against heavy competition, the single greatest weapon to winning in multiple-offer situations is *not* being the highest bidder. The answer is the 10-day close. Master it and your income will skyrocket!

FIVE

FIVE

FIVE
FIVE

Succeeding with Sellers

Between the tortoise and the hare, you know which one wins the race to get rich, don't you? Neither. Animals don't use money. However, if you apply this fable to business types you'd find that, just as with the fictional match-up in the fable, it is *indeed* the tortoise that gets wealthy *much* more often than the rabbit. Sure, there are lottery winners and the occasional entrepreneur like Facebook's Mark Zuckerberg who strike it rich, but they are the rarest of exceptions.

Do I want you to go slow! No way! I'm not implying that I want you to *work* at the speed of the tortoise. The rabbit has a role in your business, too. I want you to *work* like the rabbit, but I want you to *think and persevere* like the tortoise.

Everyone thinks they are going to beat the system. Human nature. Find a better way. Everyone believes they are going to find *the* magic loophole and figure out a way to make extra cash with no strings attached.

You're not wrong in wanting to find a better way. Tweak the establishment. Create trends. Add your own wrinkle. But my message for *Momentum* has been: don't try and *beat* the system. Instead, do your homework, then ADOPT a proven system and doggedly stick to it. Because if the stock market has shown us anything it's that consistent *stick-to-it-ness* is the way to success. And real estate is *exactly* the same way. Don't go for big, quick, easy scores. If it sounds too good to be true, it probably is. Instead, develop a system that you extract from a *proven* method — or methods — and stick to it!

In large part, *Momentum* is about my methods. Sure, there are other facets of real estate that won't get covered in this book. But I've integrated the seven major components (working with buyers, working with sellers, winning multiple offers, 10-day closes, open houses, working with and hiring staff, and building a team of agents) that, in my business, overlap and complement one another best. *Momentum* is about the lessons that I have learned both by trial and error *and* by watching and learning from others.

I could have made this book larger, but you can figure out how to save on office supplies all on your own.

But *Momentum* is not just about my successes. Nope. My sometimes *monumental failures* have also combined to help bear

> I've found out what works because I've tried things that didn't.

out the absolute truths inside the lessons in *Momentum,* as well. This book exists to teach you about how I approach my real estate business. It's an approach that I think is as good as any out there because I've adopted and integrated the lessons I've learned, the successes and failures of myself, and of other agents, along the way.

In other words, in part, *I've found out what works because I've tried things that didn't.*

Track the Market for Up and Down Trends in Pricing

So what do you do when you aren't selling and recruiting and lead-generating? The first, second, third, and fourth things you should do are to learn. I mean *absolutely* become intimately familiar with the trends and the direction of the current market. You need to track the market to figure out how to price the listing right the *first time*. Because pricing the market right the first time is essential to making your business slippery-smooth and efficient. Having to do things over and over is not a good way to run your business (or your life). In short, *I know* that you can prepare to succeed with some well-placed energy and preparation because, in a competitive market, keeping mistakes and do-overs to a minimum means that you have the best chance to survive and thrive.

Comps

So, to succeed, you need to know your market which means you have to know the trends. To do this, I utilize the MLS (Multiple Listing System) to go back over the comps for the past three months — and *only* the past three months! In a declining market a lot of agents will study comps going back six months (and some will even go back a year). But I go back 12 weeks, and 12 weeks only! (The exception would be when there are NO new sales in the previous 12 weeks. If there are no new sales, then *of course* you have to adjust accordingly. Under those circumstances you may have to go back six or even 12 months to find enough data to nail the market and understand what trends are at work).

For a solid reference point to accurately gauge pricing, I would only look at the "solds" and "pendings." When doing this you are merely looking for a story or a pattern. Say you pull up 10 or 20 or 30 sales. Sure, you should get a reasonably solid idea of the pricing after reviewing 7 sales — but don't stop there! You want more than 7, more than 10, even more than 15! The closer you get to 30 sold homes, the better.

We are businesspeople. A sharp instinct for pricing from reading the trends comes from combining your experience with as much *recent or current* data as is available. When I review 30 sales, my sense of how to price a home becomes instinctual. That may seem contradictory — instinct versus research — but *each sale, each week, and each market* is unique because you are throwing off sales from 13 weeks ago in favor of adding the most recent week. Your research findings are evolving every seven days. By "instinctual" I mean that the data is so complete that I cannot *just* estimate a price that is "close enough"; 95% of the time I can hit it right on. Because with my experience and with that much *recent* information at hand, I can predict the selling price almost perfectly. I have homes that sold for "this" much, and I have homes that sold for "that" much. And *this* is the direction the pattern is going. And *this* is the price that the home will sell for.

So why not go back even further and look at six months or a year's worth of sales? "Time" is the short answer. Real estate information gets old and stale very fast. The market changes that quickly and six months back is NOT representative of what is going on today.

But an even truer answer about sales data is that *I know my market well enough that I'm looking for mini-trends inside of trends. We are looking for microclimates.* We are looking for sales data that reflects mood and trend and probability. So, where there's a lot of activity — *for most regions of the country* — going back over 12 weeks of sales provides you with the information you *truly* need and can best utilize, *and* it's the most efficient use of your time.

Trends in Hand — Now What?

How do you further pan your stream for truly useful information? You want to eliminate fluky sales that don't fit the traceable pattern. So, if you find that three homes sold for $420,000, $425,000, and one for $460,000 — but that *after* those three sales, each close was above $500,000, right away you'll want to eliminate those three lows. They are usually the result of floods or because they backed up to the freeway. Maybe they were even neglected REOs or divorce sales trashed out of spite or anger. So throw them out!

Of course the same thing applies to the other end of the pricing spectrum as well. You also have to toss out the highest sales. They don't fit the pattern, either. Whereas neglect may have driven the sale price down for the homes in the $400,000s, let's say the three highest sales were $575,000, $600,000 and $650,000. So throw them out, as well!

Now if you're into wishful thinking, or you're one of those rare breed of working agents who refuses to trust trends in numbers, then I have a suggestion for you: go look at them. Go look at the houses. Get in your car and go look at the three properties that don't fit the pattern. Why did they get $650,000? Were there plantation shutters and upgrades galore? Is it in a gated community? Is there acreage? Horse stables? Or was it simply an impulsive buy?

You'll quickly learn that YOU ABSOLUTELY CAN TRUST THE TRENDS AND NUMBERS.

I work in the Sacramento area. Sacramento has highs because we get a lot of buyers from the Bay Area: people who *think* any house priced at $500,000 is a bargain. Yes, $500,000 in Sacramento *is* a very nice home. But what does $500,000 bring a mere 75 miles west of Sacramento in the San Francisco Bay Area? Not so much.

Still, what's your goal? You are trying to eliminate mistakes in your pricing and expedite sales. Get rid of the extremes in the margins. It might be that a Bay Area couple paid the extra $50,000 to be near their children. Or they were just a couple flush with cash from selling at *exactly* the right time.

A Warning about a Surprisingly Common Shortcut That Is Unethical and Illegal

Now, as that big, bold, attention-grabbing headline says, there is a surprisingly common — and illegal — maneuver that some people just can't seem to resist, so here's a little warning for rabbits looking for shortcuts: Early in my career I was approached by people who would say, "Pay me $600,000 and I'll write you a check for $40,000 at the close of escrow."

I understand that it seems harmless and easy. But a smart tortoise would never even *think* of doing that. And rabbits that do this type of thing either end up stewing in jail or on probation. You'll get caught, you'll be humiliated, and you'll be a criminal. Everyone doesn't cheat. And rabbits who cheat end up spending the next 30 years trying to explain the mistake that ruined their lives.

Everyone doesn't cheat.

Do not break the law, *ever*. If you do things with integrity and honesty, and you work hard, it's not that difficult to be successful — and you'll certainly feel better about the success you achieve. By going along with this scam (a kickback), or any scam, you've violated a truth-in-lending law that is very clear. You've violated a HUD 1 statute — and because the seller inflated the purchase price of his home by $40,000 — you've defrauded the buyer out of $40,000. I've seen it. Maybe you have, too. I implore you, DON'T DO THIS! And while you are at it, dump that high listing, because that just may be the reason it was that high.

Presenting the Price to the Seller

In the search for a median selling price, we are left with something between $500,000 and $550,000, with $525,000 being right in the middle (of course, you have to adjust for your particular market).

Now, generally speaking, sellers can be much tougher to work with than buyers. But they don't have to be. If you do your research and are armed with information, then working with sellers can be a breeze. Along those lines, there are some simple things you can do to control the relationship and limit friction. It may seem minor, but one thing that I *never* do is tell the seller the price of his home. Instead, I let the information "sculpt" the price. The information will do the work for you. So this is the first key to working with sellers. I utilize my research and information to *tell me* what their home is worth and then I present the seller that information.

Managing Expectations

Next comes one of the most important parts of working with sellers: managing expectations. I call this period the "setting the ground rules" stage and it is vital to your success *and* to your sanity.

After I get the listing, I tell the sellers that I will call them on Monday of every week. NOT EVERY DAY, but *every week, on Monday*. And, of course, Mondays are perfect, because sellers understandably want to know what happened over the weekend.

Let's say you have 12 listings. Before you go to lunch, or before you do anything else, you call them each and every Monday. All your listings. At the beginning of each week you call them and give them a full rundown of events and progress related to their houses. It may seem minor, and your personal style may be to wing it and pass along news as it arrives — but that is a mistake. It's a mistake because you are setting yourself up for chaos and hurt feelings. You're not into chaos, you are into control. It's an extremely important part of my business that I call my clients on Mondays. There is a rhythm to this pattern and my clients quickly grow used to it.

Now, importantly, NEVER WAIT UNTIL THEY CALL YOU! I once had a client who, after I had told him I would call him every Monday morning, he would purposely beat me to the punch and call me every Monday morning at 8:00 a.m. Months later I actually found out that he thought I was doing a bad job. Why? Because this seller felt that if he hadn't called me he would never have gotten any information.

Of course he was incorrect. But for that particular client his perception was reality. It's pretty straightforward: you cannot overestimate the power of taking the initiative in business. That bears repeating: it can be as simple a thing as being the one to make the call, but *you cannot overestimate the power of taking the initiative in business* by contacting your clients before they contact you. It's one of the few "constants" in human nature — we *love* to be sought out by the people we've put our trust in. We *love* for them to reward our faith with their competence and forthrightness. So I implore you to call your clients. Get hold of *them*. You simply must be the one who is in control for them to be confident for the other 150 hours a week that you are *not* in touch. Besides, there's a little secret here: when you initiate contact, you are on the offensive. *You* are the one who is asking the questions. *You* have the answers in hand and are not back-pedaling and scrambling for information. Plus, you are accomplishing something you said you would. Calling a client each and every Monday is an incredibly effective *and simple* way to show your client that you are a person of your word, that you are on top of your game and that you have their interests at heart.

Preparing to Make the Call — You Ask the Questions

Before I make my Monday calls to my sellers, the first thing I do is check the computer so I am prepared — and it only takes a minute. A quick check of the computer tells me all I need to know. The first thing I'm looking for is to find out exactly how many "hits" they've had on the house. A certain number of hits should result in a certain number of showings. So I check the computer and make sure the listing is getting hits.

A typical call usually goes something like this: I phone my seller and say, "How's it going? How many showings have you had?"

Because I've priced the house for the current microclimate, usually my sellers have numerous showings. Showings equal sales, because when people look, they buy.

But let's say I ask about showings and in spite of 180 hits, this particular seller says, "I haven't had any."

"Well, that concerns me. I've checked the computer and you've had 180 hits on your home, but no showings?"

"Not one."

Of course, I know that what comes next is an adjustment down. My pricing might be based on research and instinct, but it's not perfect. Anyone reading this book needs to realize that 180 hits with no showings almost certainly mean only one thing: the price is too high. But do I tell the client that? Not exactly. Instead, I *help them* tell me.

"One hundred eighty hits but no showings. That's *extremely* rare."

"Really?"

"What do you think it means?"

This is the art of selling compliance. You don't *tell* the seller what to do any more than you told them what the price of their house should be. Instead, you *provide* them with information and then provide them with an opening so they can tell you what you already know — and so they can feel pretty good about it. When it comes to hits and showings, when I make that call, it doesn't take long at all for the client to tell me that perhaps their house is priced too high.

Information Is Everywhere, You Just Have to Ask

Now, what about when you have, say, 17 hits on a house, which results in five showings, but you have no offers? Five showings and no offers? The first thing I do is ask my client for the names and numbers of the agents who showed the house over the weekend. I or someone on my staff calls the agents and asks if they are going to make an offer on the house. If they say yes, then great! Then I am the one who calls my seller with the good news. But it's when they say no that I get the true feedback I need to help my client sell his home.

"How'd you like the house?"

"Oh, it was a beautiful house."

"How was the price?"

"Oh, great price. Gr-r-reat price!"

So the agent has already told me "beautiful house" and "great price."

Sounds great, doesn't it? But let's be honest here: if you don't hear from someone after they view a house, *they probably aren't interested.* Which is 100% fine, because their interest level isn't the *only* reason I'm calling. I'm calling because those agents are all actually my partners in this process, and together we are going to expedite the selling of my client's house. Because *now* when I call, I'm not calling to see if they are interested in the house (though occasionally they are). I'm calling so they can tell me *exactly why* their buyer passed on the house.

"I noticed a pet smell."

"It needed paint."

"The neighbors stole my car."

Let's say you have a client with a house listed at $750,000, but you've gotten no offers. You call four agents who have had buyers tour the house. You ask them what they thought.

They will usually be polite and say, "Beautiful house! Loved it! It will sell!"

Then I ask them what they thought of the price.

Even agents in a hurry are usually unfailingly polite. They usually say, "Priced fine. It will sell!"

Here's where I earn my money with sellers. This is a simple but *highly* effective method for utilizing the expertise of the agent along with the impressions of the buyer. I ask the agent, "Ms. Smith, these clients are important to me and I really want to help them sell their house. If you were in a contest to win a million dollars, and all you had to do was guess the final sales price, what do you think this house will sell for?"

Remember, the agent and his clients have been out looking at houses in that price range and perhaps even in that exact area. Once you personalize it and bring the other agent "into the moment," you'll get honest and *valuable* information that will *drastically* speed up the selling of the house.

For the sake of argument, let's say that you have the house listed at $750,000, and you have four agents coming in with predictions of $685,000, $670,000, $695,000, $699,000 (maybe two of the agents also mention that the house could use a fresh coat of paint). That's a pretty good tell that not one of the agents — or their clients — believes the house is worth more than $700,000.

If you've been in real estate for a few years, you surely remember early 2009. Most everyone I know agrees that early 2009 was pretty well into a declining market. There is no evidence to contradict this, and anyone who for whatever reason tells you otherwise is mistaken. In terms of price, early 2009 was part of the free-fall.

So, we have a house listed at $750,000 with 180 hits (or 17 hits, 70 hits, or 170 hits). There have been some viewings, no offers, and four realtors giving me price points of between $670,000 and $700,000. Is this bad news, or is this good news? No-brainer, right?

Here's where I go back and tell my client, "The good news is that we tried $750,000, we tried a price point, but we got no offers."

The next step is also important. I never say "reduction." Never. I never say, "We need to reduce the price to be able to sell your house." We are not *reducing* anything. We are "adjusting." We are going to adjust the price to get the house sold for its *current* value. And we now know the current value is *not* $750,000.

Now, let's compound this a little bit. You let your client tell you that the price is too high. You then tell your client that we need to adjust the price to the "current value." But here's the monkey in the works. Rather than saying, "Let's do it," in which case you calculate the appropriate price adjustment, let's suppose your client says something to the effect of, "Well, we're rich. We aren't really in that big of a hurry to sell. We'll wait it out a year."

You must NEVER allow this to happen. I always tell my "patient sellers" that they need to rethink that philosophy. Despite 180 hits, they haven't received even one offer. No one even threw a low-ball offer at them just to see if they'd bite. This is not a good or typical sign. There is a problem — a declining market — and that problem isn't likely to go away any time soon.

So here we are in an obviously declining market and yet my client wants to wait.

I need to help them adjust their thinking because, in my book, they should be in full-blown panic mode. They should be frantic, and I tell them that if trends continue, in as little as one month they may not even get the $690,000 that seems so certain today. Things can change *that fast* and they need to know it. The larger trend is down. The micro-trend is down. And in real estate, *as much as any other business*, a bird in the hand is worth ten in the bush. You've got to get them to move or there's a very good chance they'll be left out in the cold.

This is where I ask them, "If you had sold this house in the Sacramento real estate market one year ago, what would you have gotten for it?"

Well, chances are they *not only* know their market, they also know what the neighbors on either side of them bought or sold their homes for. And the sense that the good times will last forever has tainted their logic. I ask them what they would have gotten for their house if they'd sold a year ago. They usually think for a moment and then their expression changes and I don't have to say another thing.

As for the down cycle in the Sacramento area, homes that were once priced at $900,000 were losing $20,000 a month from January 2008 to January 2009.

What I tell these clients is, "Sell now, and then rent until the market is obviously on the rise. Then buy." Don't predict trends based on blips. You've got to prepare in a way that will save you time *and* allow you to best serve the interests of your client. You go to your computer. You look at the solds and find one in the $725,000 range, and others in the $600,000 range, with the majority running between 625K and 675K. Next, you want to get rid of the lows at 600K and the high at say $725,000, and the rest all fit in between $625,000 and $675,000. *That's* the market value. Not the fluke sale or two, *the grouping*. Don't live for the flukes. Throw them out! Do your homework. An extra 15 minutes here on the comparable homes can save you three months of pain trying to sell the home because you overshot (or undershot) on your initial pricing.

When someone wants to sell, but then they don't receive the high offer they were expecting (probably based on something a neighbor said), and then the seller says, "I can wait another year or two," you've got to go into proactive mode. Not to say that there aren't exceptions, but thinking that they'll wait out this blip so that the price will rocket up is almost always a mistake. Because the above market is clearly in decline and could very well continue to decline for five or more years. So, statistically and professionally speaking, the good advice is to *sell now* unless they are prepared to wait five or even six more years.

> **In terms of pricing, what matters is only what happened in the last 12 weeks.**

And most people *definitely* don't want to wait that long.

You're at the computer researching pricing. Let's say you only see one "pending" and it's at $490,000. Pretty good price. Nice house. Then look at the "actives." And if a bunch (seven or eight or more) of agents have recently marked their houses down to the range of $475,000 to $490,000 — that means seven or eight actives all just recently marked down under $500,000.

Why would anyone pay $550,000 when the average is under $500,000?

Too often, where sellers get confused is when they've been listening to their neighbors brag, or listening to what the family on the next street over sold their house for a year ago. This is where your expertise comes in. You hang on the "solds," but you focus on the "pendings" and the "actives."

Important point: It simply *does not* matter what happened in the distant past. One year? Six months? *Doesn't matter.* In terms of pricing, what matters is only what happened in the last 12 weeks. Three months. From that 12-week analysis you can get all the information you need: averages, sale prices, direction of the market, coming sale price, activity, trends, *everything*. Do your research and price accordingly.

In the Beginning

Momentum has been written for agents of varying degrees of experience. It's been written so that just about *any* agent can enhance their business model. *Momentum* is NOT a get-rich-quick, "promise you miracles" book that guarantees you'll become a millionaire. I've presented the methods I use in my business out of order to how they might appear in more traditional real estate books. Now, there is nothing wrong with *some* of the A-Z books on real estate, but my experience has been that those books actually attempt to do too much, as they are trying to appeal to the broadest audience and so they aren't nearly as specific or concise as I like. They take the reader from birth through high school. Every word or phrase for the beginners, along with how and where to get a license, on up to building a team of agents and beyond for the experts.

You don't want to learn just one way of doing things, just one business model. You want to accumulate knowledge from numerous sources. You want to pick and choose.

When I entered the real estate business, I didn't immediately buy every available book or attend every seminar, however. I didn't do this because I would have been overwhelmed. Most readers of books about real estate already speak the language and have a license, so they are looking for ways to increase their knowledge *and* their income. They already work hard, so the best way to achieve greater success is through the implementation of new ideas and methods that augment *or enhance* what they are already doing.

But for every component of selling real estate — working with buyers, working with sellers, open houses, etc. — there has to be a beginning or a first time.

Simply, what should you do, and what should you *not* do, when you approach the seller to sell their home?

One of the biggest mistakes you can make is to approach a seller and *start* with the CMA. This is classic cart-before-the-horse thinking. Instead, I recommend that you start with your simple marketing plan. If you haven't already come up with a good, simple, marketing plan, then sit down with a yellow note pad and an experienced listing agent and say, "What can I do to sell the home?"

> **One of the biggest mistakes you can make is to approach a seller and start with the CMA.**

Basic Real Estate Marketing for Supernovas

In regard to marketing and sellers, here are some of the things that I recommend you do that will *noticeably* move your business forward. Go in with two other agents and each of you can purchase a one-third interest in a listing page — which means four, four, and four listings. If money is tight, or if you are just starting out, you buy a one-third interest in a page so instead of costing you $600 per month, it's only going to cost you $200 for what is, essentially, the same exposure as the full page. Then you can list four homes on a page that anyone, *anywhere in the universe*, can see when they go Internet shopping.

Is $200 too much? I once couldn't afford, *nor did I understand* the value of, investing in listing pages. Needless to say, I've become a HUGE marketing advocate and an even bigger fan of listing pages. Can't afford one-third of a page? Then go in with a partner on one-half of one-third of a listing page. You can get your cost down to $100 a month, *and it will be the best $100 you've ever spent!* It's pretty simple, really. You *cannot* tell me you want to get 20–30 listings (or more) in the next year and NOT be willing to spend some money on marketing.

Another idea to stimulate your business is to get a fractional interest in Homes.com or Real Estate Buyers Guide* (or whatever guide is most popular in your area or region). The emphasis here is that I want you to get a fractional interest in a page and put your face on it. The Real Estate Book† is another good one because it will attach you to over 30 terrific websites such as Military.com, Truvia.com, Google, Wall Street Journal‡, et cetera. Then, when you approach a seller as a potential client you can tell them, "Ma'am, I'm going to list your house in The Wall Street Journal, Google, Military.com, and ViewMyDreamHome.com. *Millions* of people will have the ability and the opportunity to see *your house*." Once you begin to list this way, you are beginning to think big. You are beginning to think outside the box of your neighborhood, your office, your region. And remember, you can't sell houses if you don't get the listing — so your visibility is an integral part of bringing clients to you, *and then closing them* on selecting you as their agent.

So what happens when you get more than three or four listings? Where are you going to put them all?

Obviously, when you get more than three or four clients, you can afford to spend more money for marketing. But you *have* to find a way to do this, so don't think you can't afford it. This book is called *Momentum*. It is not about what you *can't* do. Anyone can do anything I'm teaching in this book no matter what their budget or current income status. Because if you sell *one* of those listings for $500,000, you'll immediately be going

> **Get a fractional interest in a page and put your face on it.**

* http://rebuyersguide.com
† http://www.realestatebook.com
‡ http://online.wsj.com

to your own half-page. And that half-page will be doubly better than the one-quarter or one-third page. Soon, you'll be on your way to your own full page for $600 a month. And that should be your short-term goal: a full page. So when you start selling, you don't tell your new clients how you are doing it. You don't tell them how you are now selling ten houses a month. You just tell them, "I spend $1,000 a month on marketing. I'm spending money to market YOUR house, and YOUR house is going to be on over 50 websites and on my own personal listings page."

That kind of talk is heady stuff. And this approach is incredibly important to sellers because it marks you as a serious pro who knows what he or she is doing.

It amazes me, but most agents still don't know a thing about listing this way. I've listed homes on over 70 websites, and so can you. If you aren't already doing it, then you must do it *tomorrow*. Some agents put a home on only two or three websites. That's it. And most of those websites are small local sites like PlacerCountyHomes.com. I'm not criticizing them. Those agents have made an important first step forward, but it's not *nearly* enough. Sure, I list my sellers on those sites, as well. But I also list them on Yahoo* — and there are 40 million visitors a month for real estate on Yahoo!

So what about those smaller sites?

While there may be some trickle-down, the reality is that savvy buyers know that information is money, and that the available information sources are too accessible and too valuable not to both utilize *and* maximize. Throughout *Momentum* I've reminded you about the best returns for your money and this is one of the biggest:

> **Technology is by far the least expensive way to get maximum exposure.**

technology is worth its weight in plutonium. Technology is by far the least expensive way to get maximum exposure. Nothing

* http://realestate.yahoo.com

Presented by: The Brent Gove Home Selling Group

OUR MARKETING PLAN FOR YOUR HOME

- We Market Your Home on **22** Different **Internet Sites**

- We Run a Full Color Ad in **The Real Estate Book**
  - ❖ Northern California's Leading Real Estate Publication with **30,000 books** printed every four weeks and over **2000 distribution locations**

- Regarding Open Houses:　*National Statistics are 1 out of 100 buyer's find their home from an open house*

- We Order a **Virtual Tour** on Your Home.
  - ❖ A camera crew will come shoot a tour of your home and post it on the internet at viewmydreamhome.com

- We E-Mail Your Virtual Tour to **Over 3,000 Agents** in the Bay Area

A basic marketing plan will help you sell your services to home sellers.

comes close. Sure, it's only one part of your plan to sell their house, but over the years I've sold literally hundreds of houses via dozens of websites. This means that I've sold hundreds of homes by doing nothing more than posting them on websites. In fact, it not *only* sells homes — and this is important — it sells sellers on YOU! The phone rings, it's a buyer who saw my website, saw my face, read a write-up, and the deal is nearly done. And that deal leads to referrals and still more deals. You can't overstate the importance of marketing exposure.

You're a real estate agent. You are in marketing. You are a businessperson. You are going global from your desk. And part of the way to increase your business is to market *yourself* right along with your sellers. Marketing, exposure and technology is a three-for-one deal that will combine to make you money.

A Technology Anecdote

Here's a story: I have an older friend I'll call "Pat." Pat has been a sales rep in the furniture industry for almost 40 years and in that time he's had some great successes — medium-sized regional furniture chains buying his products — but he's had some lean years as well. Pat was always old-school. He came of age in the '60s and '70s before the explosion of computers and the Internet, when business was done face to face and sealed with a handshake. Hard to imagine, but Pat learned his trade at a time when, to be successful, he needed to get out of bed and get in his car and hit the road driving to the tune of 40,000 miles per year (that's 150 driving miles per business day over the course of a year).

About 10 years ago Pat and I drifted away from one another, but luckily, recently, we came back and renewed our friendship. Not long ago my family and I were invited to his house for the weekend. After dinner one night, Pat and I ventured down into his home office and sat back to talk. I'd always thought of Pat as an uncle, and in my mind's eye, his work habits and style, the idea that he would never have to change to remain successful, even though I myself don't run my business this way, the thought that Pat was out there plugging away, it always made me feel good inside.

Down in his home office, Pat was extremely excited about his computer and he turned it on and began to show me things. Well, needless to say, I was *blown away!* I've always been a big computer guy, but the Pat I knew in the past didn't even own one. Yet here we were, and here was Pat showing me things that hardly fit my image of him as old-fashioned.

His fingers working over the keys, Pat was tapping into shipping tables, showing me a program for figuring the available "cubes" to fill up tall truck containers, looking at the different deepwater ports in China and Vietnam that he could choose to ship furniture from, tapping into the port of Oakland and tracking freight departures and arrivals. Manifests. Pricing. Inventory. Containers. Pat knew which truck containers had been cleared by customs and which ones were still on hold. All that, and come to find that Pat was no longer an employee of any one particular manufacturer. He now worked with dozens of them — most of which came to him just *hoping* he would be their representative.

As surprised as I was, I was even more impressed. Pat had not *only* evolved, he'd gone global. He now had houses in several states. He had property in Tahoe and on the coast. He owned part of a factory in China — all from a guy who jokes he barely finished high school.

After a while, I became aware that Pat and I weren't alone. I turned to find his wife, Nancy, standing in the doorway of the office. Gesturing at the computer, I laughingly said, "Nancy, how did *this* happen?"

Nancy stood there for moment, smiled, and then raised a hand and rubbed the tips of her fingers together to indicate "money." She then said, "Our business changed. Once Pat realized how much he could do right here" (at his computer) "he learned everything there was to know about computers and the Internet."

This is important. It's not headline news that we live in the age of technology. It's old news, okay. Everyone reading this knows it. Every business benefits from maximizing the incredible information resources at our fingertips. And real estate is an industry that relies so much on information that, in terms of the opportunities that technology presents, you can't allow yourself to think that you are doing *nearly* enough when you post to just two or three websites.

Now in his late 60s, Pat is a guy who worked in an industry that for 50 years (or more) had very few changes. Made in family-owned factories in places like Bassett, Virginia, and Pulaski, Tennessee, the furniture was ordered, then constructed, and then it was placed on trucks with all sorts of other products such as produce, appliances, and clothing (and with no way to know when the furniture would arrive) and then driven across the country. As late as the year 2000 it could take four months (or even longer) to get a single bedroom set ordered, built, and then shipped across the country.

Now, from the moment the order is placed, all the way to the receipt of goods, it takes a mere four to six weeks to get a *full* truck container of furniture (30 complete bedroom sets) delivered to California from China. And not only is the cost of the furniture just 10% of the price it was in 1995, it's actually *less expensive* to ship a set of furniture across the Pacific than it is to ship it across the United States.

It's an unfortunate reality that furniture which was once made in Virginia is now made in Asia. But the fact is that, in terms of communication, construction, shipping, and selling furniture, it's a completely different world than it was only a dozen years ago.

Pat's a guy who, rather than become a dinosaur, changed

when his business changed. In the chaos of all that change Pat became a pioneer amongst reps. Instead of being phased out, by being one of the first in his industry to master the available technology, Pat was able to increase his income more than twentyfold.

Now, would-be reps and importers from all over America contact Pat to try and learn how to tie into giant Asian warehouses and shipping tables. Now, instead of having products in small, regional chains, Pat sells merchandise to chains that stretch across the country and even around the world. And that is because of his mastery of technology and his willingness to grow.

Technology Use in Business

If you want to succeed you have got to be willing to get uncomfortable. Both economically *and* technologically, things have changed. This chapter is about working with sellers, but it's also about modernizing your thinking, marketing yourself as a viable commodity, and learning what you can do to increase your income. To thrive, you do not need to be a computer expert, but you must master the technology that supports the real estate business, and you *absolutely* have to utilize this available technology because in the new economy just working hard isn't enough anymore.

> **If you want to succeed you have got to be willing to get uncomfortable.**

I repeated certain mantras throughout *Momentum*. One of those mantras is to endorse the use of technology to help your business thrive, because I *know* that it gives you the least expensive, *best return* for your time and money investment. You need to master the tools that support and expand your business to make more sales and more money. Take a class. Ask the children of your office-mate in the next cubicle. Ask your neighbors. Ask your kids. You need to do this because, I promise you, your competition is doing it. And I'm doing it because if Pat can change and excel, almost anyone can.

A Marketing Plan Solidifies *You* as the Expert

Marketing. *Marketing.* MARKETING. When you approach sellers, put everything else aside and start with your marketing. Become an expert in *presenting* to the seller the many tentacles of your reach, so you can illustrate to them how *your reach and expertise* helps you find buyers for their home. Show the seller what you can do for them. Show them how you are going to position their home in your marketing universe. Become an expert on what *you do*. Get former clients to write testimonials and post them. Show the sellers everything that illustrates and supports what you do. *Then*, after you've shown them your marketing plan and expertise, when you do go over the CMA, they'll listen to you because you have earned their respect and they understand that you know what you are doing.

Time and time again, the biggest mistake agents make is that they go over the CMA first, *and then* they go over the marketing plan; the marketing plan— the *very* foundation of our credibility — comes out in spurts and trickles.

If you lead with the CMA, it's already too late. The seller has shut down on you and here's why: they came to you thinking their house was worth $750,000 based on a two-year-old sale that a neighbor made, and the seller comes to you and you immediately go to the CMA and you are telling them, "Uh, no. Your house is worth only $450,000."

"We can wait. Goodbye."

You've just told them they've lost $300,000 and you might as well be a guy standing on the corner with a slide rule. You've begun the relationship with a big, giant NO, and there is nowhere to go from there.

But if you start out with the marketing, you begin by showing them how Internet savvy you are. You begin by showing them that you are the expert and that you know more than they do. You also know more than your competition. You can show them how you are going to use your marketing expertise and the dozens of resources at your fingertips to sell their home. You are the pro and you've won awards, you're #2 in your region, and you know your business. Let them read the letters and see the awards, certificates, or degrees. And if you are new to the game, let them see your Internet expertise and let them witness your marketing plan. Opening a laptop dazzles! It just does! Show them where and how you, the expert, are going to market their home. All those websites and all that reach. THEN you have their attention. THEN they are going to listen. And THEN, after you've shown them your marketing plan, you bring out the CMA to help them decide the current market value of their home.

> **Don't tell them what their home is worth; use the CMA to show them!**

That last line is important, because this way they've seen it with their own eyes. Don't *tell* them what their home is worth — use the CMA to *show them!* Show them what their home is worth and then ASK them what they think. Let them tell you, based on the CMA, that their home appears to be worth $500,000.

After You've Established Credibility

Now, the next thing I want you to do with sellers is to "step price" their home. What I mean by that is that you draw it out — you step it out — and show them the actives and the pendings. So remember, if the actives and the pendings are all under $500,000, I draw a step at $525,000, a step at $500,000, and a step at $475,000. I would say, "Normally [as in the past], your home is worth $550,000 to $525,000 based on these 'solds.' But because of these nine pending sales — all under $500,000 — the reality is that your home is probably worth about $500,000."

This is because the market — as it currently is in most of the country — is still going down. So I offer to market their house at $525,000, but I tell them that if they want to sell it fast, they may want to think about starting at $500,000 — and with that I'll feel confident telling the seller that their house will probably sell for no less than $475,000. And here's another tip: if you aren't *entirely confident* in your steps, then add a fourth step. Say $525,000, $500,000, $475,000 and the final step would be $450,000. Then you put the steps down, and put an x next to the $525,000 and $450,000 prices, and then tell them that you feel their house will sell for $500,000 — but don't guarantee it. Tell them that you'd like to try for the high step price for a few weeks and see what happens. But only list that for a couple of weeks. Some agents list a house at the highest level of the step for two months — this is a mistake! You are giving the seller the chance to make the most money, but you are paying for the marketing. If the high step doesn't create any buzz in a declining market in the first few weeks, then it isn't going to in the near future, either.

The Most Powerful Weapon in the World Is the Human Soul on Fire

Now, a final thing I do with sellers is, I express to them my enthusiasm. Being enthusiastic is my style, so it's easier for me than it might be for some, but you find your own particular professional voice when you understand that selling is about more than just numbers and price. It's also about competence. It's about honest enthusiasm. It's about positivity.

The sale doesn't start *after* you get the listing, the sale starts *before* you get the listing. Because without that house to sell, you might be the best closer on earth, the most Internet-savvy and the best informed, but you need that seller to allow you the privilege of selling their most prized possession. So tell that seller how hard you are going to work for them. Don't grovel, be a pro, but close them on all that you are going to do for them. And here's where the old-timey way that things have been done, done long before the Internet, comes into play: it's still about hard work, and so you tell them, so long as you really mean it, *because I always do*, you tell that potential client that no one will work harder or smarter for them than you will. You tell them that *you* are the best person for the listing and that you'll prove it to them over and over again. Let them know they are about to enter into business with the right man or woman for the job. I have no problem saying to sellers, "I will give my right arm for this listing." That's because I mean it. So many agents arrive and go over listing presentations but they refuse to get uncomfortable and risk rejection by putting themselves out there and making a pitch for the job.

The last time you purchased a car, what happened? If you're like me, after a while the pitch becomes the same. It's like Charlie Brown whenever the adults speak. "Wha, wha, wha, wha, wha." And why is that? Because selling cars is the type of selling that almost 100% revolves around the product. Sport rims, 400 horsepower, lifetime power-train warranty, wha, wha, wha, wha.

Those guys memorize a pitch and they throw it out 30 times a day.

But you aren't selling cars, you are interviewing for a job. Each and every time you meet a prospective client you are actually interviewing for a job, and to get that job you have to sell yourself. And no matter how much marketing savvy or how many awards you've won, you *close* that interview by selling your enthusiasm in the old-fashioned way: whether you are applying at McDonald's, IBM, or to get a listing, the *one thing* that hasn't changed is that everyone wants to hire a good worker, and you better close that seller by promising to be a good worker, and then delivering, because none of it happens without that. So tell them you love their house — and then decide to fall in love with it. Find the assets of that house that appeal to *you* and mentally focus on them as if it was your own.

> Each and every time you meet a prospective client you are actually interviewing for a job.

Look at the NBA. Professional basketball. Freakish physical talents. Everyone in that league has freakish natural talent. But only a few are truly great. The rest lack passion. You hear it all the time. *The passion combined with the natural gifts creates greatness.*

You are in a battle for your professional life. People are counting on you. You are in a battle. So stop going through the motions! *Give yourself a check-up from the neck-up* and start speaking from your heart and get passionate about what you do.

You'll enjoy it more, and you'll be better for it.

SIX

SIX

SIX

Leveraging Yourself with Staff

Most agents are a one-person band. Business cards, mailings, paperwork, showings, scheduling, phones, computers, research, listings, open houses, websites, selling and marketing — most of us do it all by ourselves.

It's a very heroic image, the one-person band. But is *all that* activity beneficial to you in any way?

Whether you are just starting out, struggling in a tough economy, or even if you are a fantastically successful agent, in this chapter there is a singular topic I want to emphasize: how you can leverage yourself with assistants to make more money in real estate.

Because you absolutely need help.

I approach the importance of hiring staff from two different directions and yet both take me to *exactly* the same place. First, on one end of the spectrum, do you want to ensure that you are able to stay in real estate through good times and bad? Survival. Real estate is, after all, your career and your livelihood, so I assume the answer is a resounding "Yes!" And second, from the other side of the spectrum, if you're already making good money, do you want to make even more money and have even more security? It simply isn't possible (or prudent) to be finished growing your business. So, either way, whether you're on top, or just starting the climb, the message is the same: you need an assistant. It's that simple. Because both the *most conservative* (staying afloat) and *most lofty* (making millions) professional ambitions are *made possible* by hiring the right assistant *today*.

The busywork that you do — the forms, the calls, the filings — make no mistake about it; these things need to be done and *done well*, because all these things are components of your success. But let's face it, that busywork is also incredibly time-consuming and labor-intensive. Doing all the busy, time-consuming work may feel noble to us control freaks, but don't kid yourself: it's a poverty mentality and nothing more. It's a *terrible* waste of your time because filling out contracts and fielding calls from office supply salespeople does *nothing* to make you money.

> **Whether you're on top, or just starting the climb, the message is the same: you need an assistant.**

Picture yourself as a race car driver, and busywork is putting the air in the tires of your car. Yes, you need the air in your tires to race your car. The air is important. Can't drive without it. But you can't actually drive your Porsche *at the same time* you are putting air in your tires, can you? Having to focus on busywork keeps you from ever reaching cruising speed. If every time you pull in for a pit stop it's *you* who has to climb out and check the air pressure, then you aren't going to win very many races.

When you sell a house, if you have to stop and do a week's worth of tire-inflating paperwork, you are *seriously* limiting your opportunities to create more wealth. Why? Because the vast majority of the busy, non-selling and non-networking tasks that keep you chained to your desk can be done by an assistant (or even by a sharp, motivated intern).

So why are you doing it?

I want you to make money, which means you must *clearly* understand what your time is worth.

Over the past year, is your time worth $100 an hour? Perhaps $200 an hour? Even $800 per hour? Or are you worth as much as $1,800 an hour? This is not about ego. Because no one really knows how much you make but you. This is about an honest self-evaluation of how much your selling and marketing time has been worth to you over the previous year. You've got to calculate how much you are *actually* making per hour worked, and then you've got to calculate how much you actually made per hour of time spent selling and marketing.

Again, you've got two *completely* different categories here. First, how much you make versus *total* hours worked. And second, how much you made in the hours you spent selling, showing, and marketing.

Confusing the importance of putting air in your tires with the skill necessary to drive the race car is a huge mistake, one that, at various times, we've all made. But you need to stop that now. As a race car driver, your job is to drive the car and win races. So it's time to accept that the opening and closing of your filing cabinet is not a part of your job — *it's part of your business,* but it's *not* part of your job.

Some of you may be saying, "I'm not ready to hire an assistant yet."

To which my answer is that despite probably not knowing you personally, I can tell you without hesitation that if you have your real estate license, and if you've sold some houses, you are almost certainly ready to hire an assistant.

My goal for this chapter is to do everything I can to convince you of that.

Figure Out What Your Time Is Worth

Have you ever earned a $15,000 real estate commission? And if you have, have you gone back to consider how much time you spent on that particular deal? If you spent 15 total hours on the *actual transaction,* you made $1,000 an hour.

Now, maybe you remember a transaction where you made $7,500. How many hours did that take? The same 15? That's

$500 an hour, which is *great* money by any standard and nothing to shake a stick at.

But because so many of us still do the busywork, we need a baseline for comparison. Let's say you are looking for listings, so you spend an entire day sending 300 letters to 300 potential clients. Do you really need to be the one spending eight hours sending those 300 letters? Printing them out from the database? Addressing them? Signing them? Yes, you want and need to have the letters sent. You want and need to send mailings and make postings and surf the web. But that's eight golden hours of opportunity wasted! Those eight hours, and each and every one of the many hours spent just like them, those have to be averaged into the $500 per hour you made on your last transaction.

You may be thinking to yourself, "Isn't sending out those 300 letters lead generation?" Of course it is. But it's secondary lead generation that anyone can do. It's not selling and it's not primary lead generation (like holding dynamic open houses). You need to focus on the aspects of your business that *only* you can do because, as you'll see, the more time you are able to spend directly selling and marketing, the faster your income will increase and the more money you'll make.

I want you to be able to focus your time doing what directly makes you the most money.

You need to realize that there are people out there looking for work who would be happy to send out those letters and free you up to make deals. There are semiretired people who would love to earn a little supplemental income; people who for $10 or $15 an hour would be happy to help you get rich. And some of these people actually know databases far better than you do! Any of them are just as capable of sending out those 300 letters, or calling the pest control company, calling roofers, calling appraisers, all the stuff we think we have to do — which you should not be doing — and they'll do it with a big, unhurried smile on their faces because *that* is what their job description is.

Poverty Thinking, Putting on Airs, Old-Timey Ways

Let's say you have a college student work for you for three hours a day, a student who needs a little part-time money and who is flexible. Say they work for you Mondays through Thursdays. So, at $50 a day for your assistant, times four days a week, times four weeks a month, this assistant is costing you $800 a month.

Here's where people who are just starting out, or who are hitting a tough stretch, think, "I can't afford $800 a month right now."

And here's where I say, "Not *only* can you afford to spend that $800, you can't afford not to."

I *clearly* remember the way it was for my parents and their peers in the business world. I remember when I was just starting out in business and anyone who told an old-timer that they had an assistant was viewed as a bigheaded jerk who was putting on airs.

That was then. That was a holdover mentality from the pre-Internet, pre-cellphone age when an assistant got you coffee, picked you up at the airport, and answered your office phone.

Going back further, 30 years ago, there was a limit to what an assistant could do. Yes, they could do the paperwork. And having an assistant gave the impression of success (which was a valuable tool in an era when projecting an image of success meant as much as it does today). In *those days* just about *everyone* who had a job worked outside the home.

But let's look at it this way: life was slower 30 years ago and opportunities for business research *virtually prehistoric* by today's lightning-fast standards. Response times, expectations, checks in the mail, everything was slower then, and an assistant was indeed often just a luxury for someone who was already successful.

At best, what I call "poverty thinking" is a nuisance, but at worst it's a destructive habit. I'm not your friend at the mall trying to convince you that you need to buy a certain pair of shoes because they match your belt. Only you know if you deserve those shoes. Only you know if you really need them.

I've spent years developing my business and many, many hours coaching agents. I've written *Momentum* to help you build your real estate business as quickly as possible but, just as importantly, as *solidly* as possible. With that in mind, having an assistant is not about luxury. I've repeatedly tried to reinforce that the lessons and ideas in this book will help you build a solid foundation for success. With both success *and security* as the goal, having an assistant is not about choice, it's a cornerstone of that foundation. It's not about having a big head or putting on airs. Having an assistant is as important

> **An assistant is a basic tool for success and not a result of being successful.**

as having a car, phone, or computer. Again, this is *not* about choice. An assistant is a basic tool for success and NOT a result of being successful. Think big, yes. But first, think logically. Having an assistant is about survival, and yet at the exact same time, having an assistant will help you thrive. In that way, an assistant is the *tires* on your sports car. An assistant is vital, important, basic, integral and necessary, and you need one right now if you are ever going to achieve and maintain the success I want for you.

I Was Terrified When I Hired My First Assistant

I very clearly remember why I hired my first part-time assistant. I was overwhelmed with busywork. I'd get some momentum by selling a house and then, *wham!* I'd have to pull over into the pit stop and spend a week doing paperwork.

I knew someone who knew someone who was looking for part-time work. I hadn't really even thought of hiring anyone as I'd only been in the game two years and I wasn't making much money. When I met this person, I told her the truth: I could afford to pay her $1,200 a month but, at that moment, I was *only sure* I could pay her for three months.

Picture that scenario: it's my first hire. I was pretty new to real estate and I was only sure I could afford her for three months. Most people would've thought, "I don't have enough money to hire someone."

Wrong.

Like a glorious lightning bolt, it dawned on me: I was missing opportunities because I wasn't able to be out doing what I, like every real estate agent, do best: selling.

I was very clear with my first assistant, and I told her that my money was limited and that I might be forced to let her go in as little as three months. But I also made certain that she knew I was serious about success. That I didn't just want to hire someone as an experiment, or just for fun. I realized that at some point in business you have to take the plunge. You have to be willing to take a leap of faith. My modest success actually meant that I was limited by a lack of time to sell and market. I knew I had to do something if I wanted to get to the next level.

And deep down, I was worried that I would never make it to that next level.

I got lucky. Lucky because she was willing to take a chance on me for three months. And lucky because I made the right choice — in spite of the fact that I had no real evidence that *having* her would make me more money — I suspected it.

My plunge can be your example. I had a sense of what an assistant could do for my business. Maybe even a dream. And she was willing to take the job because I also told her that if things took off as I hoped they would, I would give her a raise.

Well, because I easily began making an extra $10,000 a month just because of her presence, at the end of 90 days I bumped her up to full-time and began to pay her $3,000 a month.

Once more: That's $10,000 more *each month* because of my assistant.

There's a lot of hype in the world, but that's not an exaggeration in any way: I learned very quickly that having an assistant was that valuable.

How did I do it? How did she do it? Simple. You've heard the saying, "You have to invest money to make money." She was better on the computer than me, quicker with email, better with services, and was able to handle 70% of the phone calls that in the past I would have had to answer or return. All of these things sapped my momentum and took me away from listings and selling: the very things I do best. The very things that *directly* make you and me money.

Not everyone is comfortable with hiring someone to do the work that, up until now, they themselves have been doing. It's a poverty mentality to fool yourself into believing that just being busy will make you money and ensure your success. That's a prime question in business: Are you busy? Or are you *productive?*

Sitting in the office until midnight every day doing paperwork and returning emails doesn't help you make money. You can put the perfect amount of air in your tires, and check it 1,000 times, but it won't help you win races. You can't win if you're not in the race. And you've got a better chance of winning a race by driving with flat tires than by not driving at all.

> **You've got a better chance of winning a race by driving with flat tires than by not driving at all.**

Cost Versus Unemployment

I'm constantly surprised by people saying, "I can't afford an assistant." Sometimes, the first thing that pops into my head is "And you'll never be able to until you hire one."

If a listing needs to be taken, then I'll often do that. But otherwise, I have my assistant do just about everything. Everything, that is, until an offer needs to be written. And, in time, if they are licensed, they can even write those. I made an extra $120,000 the first 12 months I had an assistant. But if you're asking, "Was my dramatic increase entirely due to my assistant?" Then I'd have to say, "Not entirely."

I had been gearing up in other ways and honing my business knowledge. But guess what? Had I known what it would mean to me in terms of extra income and production, I'd have hired an assistant a full year earlier. That's right! I'd have hired an assistant right at the start of my second year in real estate. No matter. I caught on. Because it wasn't just that first year and that first extra $120,000 that she helped me make. It was the second and even third extra $120,000, which continues on to today.

You can believe that I was ready to make that money, so that's why I hired her. And in one way, that's true: I didn't know any better and so I waited longer than I should have. But remember: I had a budget, and I found that I knew I could afford her part-time for three months. If I had to, I would have taken an advance on my credit card to afford her. Why not give it a shot? I was obviously not making big money, not yet. But I was determined to. And I saw what could be done at the exact time that I also realized that I was standing in my own way. I was holding *myself* back. My seemingly noble desire to take a hands-on approach to every detail kept me from selling and acquiring as many new clients as I did once I was simply able to let go and delegate.

I'm here to convince you that a properly utilized assistant can make you more money in more ways than you could ever imagine. You'll have more free time to enjoy your family. You'll have less stress. You'll have a teammate. You'll have fewer sleepless nights worrying about meaningless odds and ends and tasks. And here's one of the bright little secrets that having an assistant will reveal to you: aesthetically, just like in the good ol' putting-on-airs days, your clients will respect you more, because, first, you're successful, and second, there will always be a person — not voicemail — but *an actual person* for callers to speak to. Someone who will know the answers to many of your client's questions. Someone who can expedite turnarounds and eliminate duplicate phone calls. Your assistant will know the number of the contractor. He or she will have a copy of the contract right there on their desk. When you go on vacation and a client calls? *Boom!* A person. When you are traveling for business, working with other clients, or home sick with the flu? *Boom!* An actual person: someone for clients to vent to or confide in.

The better the assistant, the better you look.

I'm passionate about real estate, success, and building businesses. And I passionately want to challenge you — the reader, the agent — I want to challenge you to NOT be a one-man band. To NOT be a one-woman band. For a hundred years, residential real estate was mainly a mom-and-pop enterprise. But if you were an attorney, a sports agent, or a high-level financial planner, you had an assistant. The entrepreneurs who succeed at the highest levels have personal assistants. And if you want to be successful, then you need one, too.

How to Hire and Who to Hire

The title "assistant" doesn't conjure up a very demanding picture, but that's a gross distortion. You want a Gal or Guy Friday. When you decide to make this important first hire, don't just hire anyone. By that I mean, don't hire a friend or relative or your best friend's sister. Don't hire your neighbor. This may well be the most important hire of your entire career. Repeat: your first assistant may well be the most important hire of your *entire* career. It both sets you in motion *and* it sets the stage going forward. It has the effect of making you more serious about what you do and how you do it.

> Your first assistant may well be the most important hire of your entire career.

Simply, you'll never have to stop and put air in your tires again.

So here are some surprising standards for your first hire: you want an assist-maker. To use an example taken from the game of basketball, you want a point guard who likes to pass more than score. You want a pass-first point guard working for your team. Someone who is nurturing and detail-oriented. Someone who gets joy out of making you look good.

The right choice in hiring an assistant can often be decided or determined every bit as much by *how* you hire them as *whom* you actually hire. And I must emphasize the following: when it comes to hiring an assistant, you are not looking for a realtor. Again, *you are not looking for a realtor.* It's extremely important to get that into your head, because you will be tempted.

You are looking for a personal assistant. You are looking for someone who can *thrive* as a personal assistant. Someone who is both task-oriented *and* customer-service-oriented. I want my assistant to be good with people and GREAT with me. I want them to learn what my needs are and what makes me a better agent, which in turn makes me money and gives my assistant job security. Donald Trump and Warren Buffet and a million lesser-known moguls all hired assistants with their first *real* hire.

> When it comes to hiring an assistant, you are not looking for a realtor.

Love the DISC (assessment)!

I speak about them at length in Chapter 7, "How to Build a Team of Agents," but I'm also going to write about the *incredible value* of DISC personality assessments here as well. Because the actual *hiring* of people is both a critically important *and* extremely difficult component of business, you want to do absolutely *everything you can* to reduce the risk of a bad hire.

Here's how:

To avoid bad fits, make certain you have *every* applicant complete an easy-to-administer, inexpensive DISC assessment. A DISC assessment is a very simple, 24-question exam that will give you 19,000 different personality responses resulting in 382 personality types.

So, what exactly is a DISC assessment? First, DISC is an acronym that stands for:

Dominance – relating to control, power, and assertiveness
Influence – relating to social situations and communication
Steadiness – relating to patience, persistence, and thoughtfulness
Conscientiousness — relating to structure and organization

The purpose of these assessments is to predict the behavior of individuals in their work environments. The assessment measures the intensity levels of four particular personality traits (dominance, influence, steadiness, conscientiousness) that all people have.

Simply, you pay a small fee (about $25), and the applicant sits down and completes the assessment (it takes just a few minutes), and then the answer sheet is faxed to the administering company, which emails you the results, usually the same day. (You can also have applicants take DISC assessments online.) The results are easy to read and understand (and are explained in detail) and will show you if the applicant is a good or bad personality fit for the job you are looking to fill.

Now, because they've been so good to me, an enthusiastic DISC assessment endorsement is in order: they flat-out work! And for those of you who don't believe in standardized assessments in any way, shape, or form, that's fine. Non-adherents probably aren't reading *Momentum,* anyway. A small aside would be that while I *deeply* believe in the value of DISC assessing (it's very tempting to call them "tests" — which I often do), they are in no way a traditional test in that there is no pass or fail, and no actual grading. DISC assessments don't tell you if someone can add or subtract or file or spell. They tell you what the person is going to be like to work with and how they will handle interactions on the job. Simply, they immediately tell you the *one thing* that otherwise would take weeks or months to figure out: does the applicant have the proper mentality for the job?

Of course, this doesn't mean that DISCs are my only means of picking assistants or agents for my firm. In a fast-paced work environment, where people and applicants come and go, you

Name: _____   Male _____ Female _____   Date _____

Personal Concept

READ CAREFULLY: Complete the information at the top. Please print your name clearly. In each of the three columns below there are eight four-word groups. Select two words in each group of four words—<u>one word</u> which is <u>MOST</u> like you and <u>one word</u> which is <u>LEAST</u> like you.

EXAMPLE: AUTOCRATIC [X]
CONGENIAL
STABLE [X]
EXACTING

M L		M L		M L
EXPRESSIVE		HIGH-SPIRITED		ADVENTUROUS
COMPLIANT		TALKATIVE		ENTHUSIASTIC
FORCEFUL		GOOD-NATURED		ADAPTABLE
RESTRAINED		SOFTSPOKEN		LOYAL
STRONG-MINDED		CONTENTED		HUMBLE
CAREFUL		IMPATIENT		GOOD LISTENER
EMOTIONAL		CONVINCING		ENTERTAINING
SATISFIED		RESIGNED		WILL POWER
CORRECT		RESPECTFUL		LIFE-OF-THE-PARTY
PIONEERING		GOOD MIXER		OBEDIENT
EASY MARK		AGGRESSIVE		TOLERANT
INFLUENTIAL		GENTLE		COMPETITIVE
PRECISE		POISED		CAUTIOUS
DOMINEERING		CONVENTIONAL		NEIGHBORLY
WILLING		NERVY		VIGOROUS
ATTRACTIVE		ACCOMMODATING		PERSUASIVE
EVEN-TEMPERED		CONFIDENT		RESERVED
STIMULATING		COOPERATIVE		OUTSPOKEN
FUSSY		ARGUMENTATIVE		STRICT
DETERMINED		RELAXED		ELOQUENT
TIMID		RESTLESS		OBLIGING
DEMANDING		WELL-DISCIPLINED		ANIMATED
PATIENT		INSPIRING		DOGGED
CAPTIVATING		CONSIDERATE		DEVOUT
OPEN-MINDED		DIPLOMATIC		ASSERTIVE
COMPANIONABLE		COURAGEOUS		GREGARIOUS
KIND		SYMPATHETIC		NONCHALANT
SELF-RELIANT		OPTIMISTIC		DOCILE
AGREEABLE		EAGER		OUTGOING
SELF-CONTROLLED		POSITIVE		BOLD
PLAYFUL		LENIENT		MODERATE
PERSISTENT		EXACTING		PERFECTIONIST

Hunter-Wells International, 115 Fifth Green Court, Atlanta, GA 30350   Ph: 770-640-7740
©Copyright Hunter-Wells International 1976, rev. 2005   Fax: 770-640-9917

DISC Personal Concept reprinted with permission of Hunter-Wells International.

are likely to be continuously evaluating prospective employees who are complete strangers to you. The relatively small amount of time you spend with applicants over the course of the hiring process is too often not enough to accurately gauge who exactly you are dealing with. Simply, some people interview extremely well, but can't do anything else. Time at work, the stress of the job, multitasking, issues at home — these factors and thousands more, they all affect the output and performance of employees.

It's important to reassure applicants that a DISC assessment is nothing for them to fear. It's not an IQ test and no one comes out looking bad. Someone may actually assess-out that they would be a perfect CEO of a corporation but not a great assistant. Tell them that, because that's what the DISC assessment does: helps you find people with the best disposition for the position you are looking to fill.

They are that good and they are that easy.

There are some more expensive personality assessments (the 100-question Myers-Briggs, for one) and I've tried them myself. These can cost as much as $200 or even $300, and frankly, they are worth it as well (and what's $200 if you make a good hire?). But my experience has shown me that the shorter DISC assessments are just as powerful as the longer, more detailed, more expensive models, and that these shorter versions will give you a comprehensive look at both the "adaptive" or learned personality of the applicant, and the "natural" personality of the applicant (who people really are versus how they act in an interview). These shorter versions will also show you which traits will surface over time and become dominant and how that will affect and define their work.

What Results Am I Looking For?

Some personality types are better aligned to certain jobs and careers than others. Some people will thrive in fast-paced work environments and in concert with the personality types of their coworkers, while some types won't. I cover what I want from my team of agents in Chapter 7 (here's a hint: my agents' personalities are 180 degrees opposite from what I want in assistants). But I want my assistant applicants to grade out "dominant" in the S and C categories of the DISC assessment (steadiness and conscientiousness) because S and C personality types are the most organized and tend to love lists and predictable work environments. Not surprisingly, they also tend to be more intuitive and more concerned about the needs of others.

As an aside to what I want in an assistant, I like to think of automobile mogul Henry Ford. Ford invented the modern, moving assembly line. He was considered, by the other moguls of the day, to have only average intelligence. Now personally, I doubt Henry Ford had only average intelligence, but I have read a lot about Ford, and what he freely admitted was that he had a poor memory and that he was not overly organized — he was obviously a big thinker who clearly understood his strengths and weaknesses.

To compensate for his shortcomings he hired brilliant, organized assistants and staff, and they helped him accomplish his goals and dreams (and aren't we all better for it?).

Now, I'm not very organized and I know it. I tend to misplace things and overschedule. And if I don't have someone to help me keep my schedule, I consistently run late. So, does that mean I'm unintelligent? By some people's standards, I am (I was an average student in school). But I believe one of the reasons I've excelled is that pretty early on in my professional career I became aware of my weaknesses. It was important to me to improve and so I worked hard to try to be better organized. But, in the end, it's the people that I've hired who've made sure that I'm on time. It's my hires that have made me strong where I was weak or lacking.

There's Someone Sitting Over There – What Now?

Right after you hire an assistant and train them a little, you'll probably find yourself twiddling your thumbs for half a day. Okay, twiddle. But after a few hours, you'll realize, "Hey, I've got a lot of time to fill. Better go get some business." A whole new world of opportunity is going to open up for you. A whole new perception of what you can do to make money. Because how many times have you said to yourself, "If I only had more time" or "If there were only more hours in a day"?

I'm guessing probably thousands and thousands (especially if you're a parent). Well, if you take the plunge and make the right hire then you've just given yourself the equivalent of more hours each day to market, sell, and create *real* business and profit.

Everyone will develop their own style that helps them manage an assistant, but if you haven't had one before, here's what I would do to make the transition as smooth as possible: first, keep a simple yellow notepad close by you at all times. This yellow pad is strictly for managing your assistant. Spend five minutes before you go to bed (or when you are driving down the road) thinking of things for your assistant to do, and then simply jot them down. This is his or her to-do list. I may call her if I think of something urgent, and there are certainly going to be tasks that your assistant does each and every day, but I write down things that come to me and I tear off the yellow piece of paper and I fax it, or give it to her directly. She then crosses them out and leaves me a note if there is anything further to be done, or any information that needs to be passed along. It's simple, but it's also effective. And while it may seem obvious, it's imperative that you begin to fill that new influx of time with the pursuit of listings and selling.

Guess what? Now there are two people working hard with the same exact goal.

Still not sure that you can keep your assistant busy?

Of course you can. And if you struggle, it's only because of inexperience and a lack of very simple planning on your part. Get to the office before your assistant, grab each file you are working on, and ask yourself what needs to happen in that file to make it complete. ANYTHING and everything that can be delegated *should* be delegated. To be effective you've got to give up the part of you that is a control freak for simple, mundane tasks. "Tasks" are no longer your concern. Later on you will develop systems that put your escrows on autopilot and you in command. But the older I get, the more I've come to learn that *real* control comes from giving it away.

> Anything and everything that can be delegated should be delegated.

An assistant with free time is an assistant with the opportunity to make my business grow. An assistant with free time is an assistant who is cold-calling. In their free time, your assistant should be calling the local banks and asking if you can be recommended to their clients who've gotten pre-approved for loans. Your assistant should have a list of local banks, and once every two to three weeks, they should call those banks and ask for an appointment for you. Many banks will say no at first. But plenty will say, "Yes, come on down." They'll give you the opportunity to make a pitch to be their realtor of choice. And this comes with the added bonus that, when you become — or agree to become — the realtor of choice for a bank, you, in turn, make them "your bank of choice," because you are meeting lots of people from out of town who are relocating to the area, and they all need a bank.

You'll need to make sure to remind them of that.

How about mailers? Monthly or quarterly, every time you get a client, you can have your assistant prepare the disclosures. Another thing for assistants to do when they have downtime is to call the relocation departments at the larger local firms and companies. Nearby where I live in Sacramento, we have Intel, Hewlett Packard, and Pac Bell, just to name a few. We had an agent in my firm recently secure the brigadier general of the local United States Army base, and that contact resulted in over 100 sales simply because of that one contact.

One hundred homes? *That's awesome!*

The businesses your assistant calls don't have to have 80,000 employees for them to be worth your time. What about builders? Have your assistant call the local builders, ask for a chance to meet them, and if it doesn't work out once, then of course you stay on them. A builder who builds 100 homes a year is an opportunity for 100 new clients each and every year. And these are just some of the things your assistant can do in their downtime. *Create business for you!*

Now, many of you reading this have probably never thought to outreach like that, and one of the reasons is that you aren't willing to spend the $15 an hour to hire an assistant. Outreach to relocation specialists and banks are just two ways an assistant can bring you lots and lots of business and subsequently pay for themselves many thousands of times over in a very short time. They just go down the list, call, and say, "Mrs. Smith would like an appointment to be your relocation specialist."

And you know what? They are legitimately impressed because you have an assistant calling them. You are out working and your assistant is in the office supporting you and helping to make your business multidimensional. They *know* you are not a fly-by-night realtor who is too lazy to go out and work. They will assume that you are a serious bidder for their partnership just because you have an assistant making your appointments.

Without an assistant, you are a one-person band and, in my opinion, not likely to take your business to the next level. You need someone to do the busy stuff. You need someone to do the outreach. You need someone to answer the phone and return sales calls. But most of all, you need someone to put the air in the tires of your race car. The day you return to the office to find, not only all your files organized and your paperwork complete, but a series of new leads generated by your assistant's calls, is the day you slap yourself on the forehead before patting yourself on the back. You are about to make more money. Hire correctly and carefully. If you commit to hiring an assistant, then do your due diligence so that you hire the *right* assistant. Hire an assistant and hire well. You'll drive longer, you'll drive faster, and you'll win more races than you ever imagined.

SEVEN

How to Build a Team of Agents

I'm very proud of the fact that most of the realtors and brokers that I know work extremely hard. After all, we don't work for the government, we work for ourselves! Real estate is serious business, and it can be tough. So, understandably, maybe you yourself feel that in terms of available time and energy you're already maxed-out.

You're not alone.

So, how do you better utilize the hours you already invest in real estate — how do you get more money out of the hours you already work — and yet still balance your priorities? God? Spirituality? Family? Health? Business? Winning your fantasy baseball league?

And, as an aside, what if you're a beginner? What if you're a beginner and you're looking for lessons about how to make your business grow?

As it relates to this chapter, the amount of experience you have in real estate really doesn't matter. It's nothing like Chapter 6, "How to Leverage Yourself with Staff." Just about anyone who has been in real estate for a year or more is ready to hire an assistant. But a team of agents? I hope that by the time you've finished reading this chapter you'll know if you are *truly* ready to take the plunge (or not). And even if you aren't ready, this chapter should serve as a guideline to let you know when you will be ready. Simply, whether you're just starting out or whether you are #1 in your region, it's all the same: you're here to learn and I've got something to teach you.

So, maybe you already have an assistant. You have experience and your business is good. Perhaps 30, 40, or even 50 houses sold-per-year good.

After you have experience, after you've learned the ropes and the business of real estate, the *surest* way to make *more* money in real estate is to build *and maintain* a team of agents who, in exchange for your experience and training, will sell homes and split the commissions with you.

If you work in a luxury-home market, you can make a lot of money by selling 10 or 15 houses per year. Not *only* is there nothing wrong with that, if that's your story and you're satisfied with it, I say, "Congratulations!" But no matter what your market, and no matter what your income, there are financial and tactical advantages to having a team of agents working for you that you'll never be able to realize if you work alone.

First, it's not all about the money. It can't be. While I've spoken throughout *Momentum* about *increasing* your income, it's not all about money. No one that I know who doesn't like what they do for a living can maintain a level of success, or interest, for very long (at least not without making everyone around him or her absolutely miserable). If you've been practicing real estate for a while, then one huge asset in your pocket is that you've accumulated knowledge that has value. So hiring a team of agents, and building a team, means you get to share your knowledge with the agents you hire in exchange for a percentage of their sales. Simply, in both the short and the long term, you are going to improve the lives of the people you hire while they learn from you. You're also going to have the thrill of succeeding as the leader of a team. For me, one of the biggest thrills in business is when I get the opportunity to teach, train, and consult. So it's no coincidence that, in return for my knowledge, inexperienced agents become great agents a whole lot faster. Let's face it, that's what I want! And even though it's *exactly* what I want, we have a lot of fun doing what we do, together, as a team. And *that's* something else that I very much want as well.

Most anyone who has any experience in real estate wants to know how to build a team because a well-run, well-trained team working together makes money.

But nothing *that* important (success) comes without hard, smart, diligent work. This may sound like a broken record, but I don't care. I recommend that you become educated in every aspect of real estate available to you. Listen, read, subscribe, and learn. What's so bad about it? No fear. Listen and learn from those you want to imitate, but just as importantly, listen and learn from agents whose businesses are vastly different from yours. Make up your mind that you're never going to stop being open to learning, which means you have to be willing to listen.

> Make up your mind that you're never going to stop being open to learning, which means you have to be willing to listen.

That's a cliché. I get that. But it's also 100% true: someone always knows more than you. That's okay! I attend seminars and read at least two business or real estate books just about every month. The person that knows more than you is not your adversary. To the contrary, he or she is your ally. He or she is your friend. Learn from them. This means you have to take a bite of humble pie and ask questions. This means you need to attend seminars, listen to educational CDs, subscribe to worthwhile newsletters, study the experts, memorize the trends, and learn the nuances of your trade. Because both directly and indirectly, everything you do to educate yourself about real estate will pay off over time. Everything.

In short, be determined to be learning-based!

Everything About *Momentum* Is Fast, Except This

Want to build a team? Where time after time I encourage you to speed boldly ahead in every other facet of real estate — be brave, plunge in, and risk embarrassment rather than hold back and wait for the perfect opportunity to present itself — when it comes to building a team by hiring agents, there is something I absolutely encourage everyone to do first. And frankly, it's a *must*. Before you build a team, before you hire other agents to work for you, there is something you must first accomplish.

Success.

That's right. You need to be successful *before* you attempt to build a team.

A good benchmark for when to begin team building is when you've reached the point where you are consistently selling two to three homes a month. Keep that pace up for a year and the odds are decent that you are qualified to enter the teaching phase of your business.

Everyone has different styles. You may teach by example, or you might teach by using a carefully crafted lesson plan — which you *always* follow up by sensational *and moral* mentoring. But if you are able to sell two to three homes per month in an ongoing manner, in most circumstances, it's a pretty good bet that you know what you are doing and are ready to move on to the next step in real estate: team building.

Congratulations!

It's pretty simple: if you are achieving a consistent level of success over an extended period of time (one year minimum), you *absolutely* have something to offer a team of agents. And if you then make the right hires? They *absolutely* have something to offer you.

But first, a warning:

We live in a fast-paced world where people are encouraged *and trained* to put the cart before the horse. With access to the

Internet, everyone's become a minor-league expert on everything. (Have you ever actually had someone tell you that your doctor doesn't know what he or she is talking about?)

What's your background? Are you a college wunderkind and a natural salesperson? Or have you been in marketing for 30 years and are just now switching your career to real estate? Either way, six months tearing up the local market is fine. That's great! Congratulations! You should feel proud. But you need a lot more success than that if you are going to build *and maintain* a successful team that meets your needs, *and their needs*, for the long haul. You simply need more success than six months tearing up a hot market before you take on the responsibility of managing yourself, your business, your assistant, and your team. Otherwise, you'll lose it all before you know what hit you.

How Bad or Premature Hiring Hurts You

The most common error that I see lead agents make is when they neglect to get a rock-solid time commitment from the agent *before* they hire. I'm not beating around the bush. I'm team-building. So when I bring an agent on board to work on my team, right up-front I ask them for a four-year commitment. Four years. It never varies. I make this very clear.

> **I ask all new agents for a four-year commitment.**

Does four years seem like a long time? The only reason a four-year length of commitment should *ever* concern you is if you aren't ready to lead.

I explain to my new agent hires that I'm preparing to invest two years of my life in training them. In the course of the two years that I spend training someone, I spare no expense and I hold nothing back. In fact, I do such a thorough job — and give them the keys to every room in the castle — that I fully realize *and expect* that in two years they will feel like they don't need me anymore.

That's excellent! The feeling that they no longer need me means just one thing: I've done my job. I've raised them up in the business. I've successfully transferred my knowledge base to them. And right at that time — around two years — there's a natural tendency for them to think "I'm ready to rock and roll on my own!"

It's human nature. So I tell them up-front, *before they are hired*, with absolute clarity, I tell them that if they are coming to work with me that I expect a four-year commitment. I explain to them that, at the two-year mark, just when it *finally* gets easier (and financially viable) for me, that they'll want to leave and take all my effort and energy with them.

They usually shake their head no. And I appreciate that. But I also understand human nature. There's no duplicity there. They mean it when they say no. Right at that moment they want to make it work forever.

But for them to leave me after two years of intensive training would be both bad business and unfair to me.

So I ask them to meet me halfway. I tell them that if I am going to hire them, then I will give to them two years of intensive training, and in return for that training they will need to give me two years of hard work and production in return.

And those are the *only* terms that I am willing to mentor an agent by.

It's nonnegotiable.

At this point in *Momentum* I think it bears stating that in my *entire* career selling real estate and leading a team of agents (almost 14 years), I've had only two agents agree to those terms and then break their commitment (before our four years was complete).

That's not bad: two agents. Things happen. But about 98% of my new hires have stayed the four years, and that's what I like to focus on: Retention. Longevity. Working relationships that have value to all interested parties. *That's* what makes hiring new agents worthwhile. And I'm more proud of that 98% retention statistic than any other standard or landmark that I've achieved, *including* the number of homes sold or total commissions made.

How Do You Build a Loyal Team?

My first advice is very, very simple, but I'll repeat it, because it may be the most clear-cut part of *Momentum*. Before you build a team of agents, first, you MUST become successful. Experience is irreplaceable. You can't fake it. I know you want to build your empire as fast as possible, but you have to be worth following into battle. Be aware that no matter what your style or your particular talent, if you put the cart before the horse and haven't already achieved a reasonable and *sustained* level of success (i.e., you know the answers to just about every question you'll be asked), one morning you'll arrive at the office and everyone will be gone. Or worse, your business will bleed to death with constant turnover and wasted opportunity. So be successful. Don't try to fake it. You can't. Become an expert. Earn respect by knowing what you are doing (and you can *greatly* speed this process up by being learning-based).

That's my first nugget. You may be saying, "Well. That's just great. I want to be successful at real estate and build a team, and now he's telling me that I can't be successful at real estate and build a team until I'm already successful at real estate."

Oh, do I have a story for you.

I have a friend who is a writer. Once people find out what he does for a living just about everyone tells him how much they want to be writers, too.

Creativity is wonderful!

There is just one problem with many of these would-be authors: a large majority of the people who stop him and tell him how much they want to be writers have never *actually* taken the time to sit down and write anything themselves.

Sounds completely ridiculous, doesn't it?

As for me? I don't think it's expecting too much to feel that someone who says they want to be a writer should have already taken the time to sit down and write something. How else would they know if it's even something they want to do?

When you fail in real estate, you start again. You move on to the next deal. Because if you really want to be in real estate — if you want to make a career out of it and earn a lot of money — at some point you're going to want to build a team, so you'd better start selling, educating yourself, and learning the business. There is no other way.

The reason I wrote *Momentum* is because, like my friend the writer, people pretty regularly come up to me at seminars and conferences, and either they ask how they can get *into* real estate, or they ask me how they can take their business to the next level. I tell them that the Nike commercial had it right: Just Do It. There's no other way. Success leaves clues. So follow someone you want to emulate. Study. Ask questions and model successful businesses. Practice. It's that simple even if sometimes it's really seems hard.

Some of the people who approach me at seminars want something *other* than the lessons I'm there to teach. Simply, *some* of these people want *everything*. Like people who fantasize about writing, or batting cleanup for the New York Yankees, others fantasize about making lots of money. I don't know why, but real estate seems like an easy way to achieve that goal.

People want to know the trick to being a writer. Some people see published authors as possessing a secret that allowed them to write their book and become rich and famous. And just like that, people want to know the trick to making money in real estate.

I'm not judging, but those people always make me smile. They make me smile because I was one of them. I was one of them when it came to the game of golf. Oh my, did I want more than anything to beat my older brother at golf. I used to ask every scratch golfer I'd meet to tell me how they became great at that game. They always sort of laughed whenever I asked them that. And you know what? Dozens of rounds of golf, and hundreds of hours of practice later, I'm getting pretty good at golf myself. I can even beat my older brother.

You want to build a team? Get busy being successful at real estate. There is no magic formula. And there is no team building without getting to work and having success. Work hard, learn the nuances of the business by reading books, attending seminars, and trying new things. Be open and creative at the same time you are learning and working. If you do these things — and really, it's simply a mindset, a decision, that you are going to be open to learning — in time, you'll actually be able to teach what you know to other agents. And *then* you'll have the secret formula that allows you to be successful and lead a team.

I once was a pretty poor college student who didn't particularly like to study. I didn't like to read, either. Not surprisingly, my grades were average.

I'm not proud to say that I never earned even one A grade in any course I took in college.

Yet, as a new agent, one day I went to the bookstore to look at real estate books. I bought one. I sat down in the coffee shop and much to my shock I read the entire book in one sitting.

I had never read an entire book in one sitting before.

From that moment on, I began to read every book I could get my hands on about real estate, but I also began to read books about how millionaires ran their businesses. And this was *long before* I made $100,000 in a single year.

> **You can learn from their trials and you can study their success.**

Soon, I began to make money.

Now I love to read.

And now I read — not just about millionaires — I read about how billionaires built their companies. I read about their successes *and* their failures. From Henry Ford to Dale Carnegie to Henry J. Kaiser to Bill Gates, *then* and *now* you can learn from their trials and you can study their success. I believe in this. It never goes out of style. They've been there. Study success (and failure) at every turn, because I guarantee you can always learn more. You can always learn more, because both success *and* failure leave clues that you can learn about and improve from.

I wrote *Momentum* with real estate and learning in mind. I wrote it to help you learn. No matter where you are in your career, I *know* there are many valuable lessons for you in these pages. There is something valuable to learn in every single chapter of this book no matter what rung of the real estate ladder you currently occupy.

Choose Wisely, My Friend

As a realtor, I got to a place where I was selling 48 homes a year before I began to build a team. I'm not a patient person, but I still did this for two full years before I considered bringing on other agents. Forty-plus homes a year for two years. So, when I say "success," I mean that *in most markets* — and I've studied many of them — you should be selling 24–40 homes a year (or more) before you consider building a team.

Now, by "team" I'm not talking about the sort of team that all agents have. I understand we all have a group of people consisting of mortgage brokers who prequalify clients, home inspectors we trust, home stagers with talent that we can count on, contractors with incredible skills, along with handymen and title and escrow officers. We all have *that* team or we're not selling anything.

I'm talking about the type of team that takes your business, and you, to the next level. I'm talking about a business where, even though *you personally* didn't sell a single house in a month, you still earned $10,000, $20,000 or even $30,000 in net profit. Now that's my idea of a team! And that team is centered *and dependent* on the proper hiring and training of buyer's agents that, like my team did on a recent weekend, grow into agents who earn you $20,000 in commissions in two days (which will make for great Mondays!).

The key is to have the interests of your partner agents (buyer agents) at heart. They *must* feel and know and understand that what you are providing for them is equitable. They must feel that they are getting something important and lasting out of the bargain. Train them, help them, *bleed* for them if necessary. It's called "servant leadership," which is the exact opposite of "big shot" real estate.

The Speed of the Leader Determines the Pace of the Pack

Sometimes agents call me, people I don't know and have never met, and we talk about real estate. As this book will attest, I'm a huge advocate of reasonable sharing. I don't keep secrets. I'm a big fan of free exchanges of knowledge and ideas. I'm not a squirrel hiding his last nut! I believe there's plenty of love and success to go around. With that in mind, my advice is to share the knowledge that you have because it will come back to you. Be a giver! Help someone else achieve success! Make a difference in someone else's life by sharing your knowledge, and by listening *carefully and intently* when they share their knowledge with you. It's a two-way street. The more I give, the more I get. When you think you're the Big Deal, you're through! Your goose is cooked. Because nobody likes working for an arrogant team leader — and they will justifiably leave you hanging when you are most in need.

One of the best ways to teach someone is by showing. I teach my agents not *only* in the office, I teach in the field, as well. Anyone who works for me, or anyone who *has* worked for me, knows the inside of my car very well. In fact, listings, seminars, open houses, meet-and-greets, I pack them in and away we go.

An old friend named Coleman taught me many years ago the lesson of "Hear one, see one, done!" You "tell" them. You "show" them. Then you let them do one. You then continue to repeat the process until they get it.

As a lead realtor, if you aren't turning away business, but you are selling roughly two or three homes per month, and you think that adding an agent will increase your business, you are probably mistaken. If you are selling three homes a month, and not turning away business, then the agent you hire will probably be given leads you would have converted yourself. By doing this you lose 50% to 60% of your commission. Only give out a lead if you cannot handle it yourself. Only then are you actually making additional revenue.

But let's say you're successful and business is good. You're turning away listings. You hire your first agent. Remember, you're the lead dog, and they are going to follow you. And while your agents are there to learn from you, even more importantly, I'm sure you'll find that they move at the pace you set. Remember: the speed of the leader determines the pace of the pack! Do you want a fast-moving, high-producing team? You set the pace. For example: if you sell 48 homes a year, a good estimate would be that your agents will sell 15–20 homes annually. But if you sell just 15–20 homes per year? They will likely close 5–10 sales annually, which is just enough to frustrate them *and you.*

> **Remember: the speed of the leader determines the pace of the pack!**

Manage Your Expectations, Manage Theirs

When an agent joins a team they are often thinking, "Hey, I'll join this team for 6–12 months, maybe 18 months. I'll learn everything I can learn and then I'll leave and start my own business."

There's nothing wrong with those thoughts. It seems like good business. Frankly, I thought the same thing when I was new.

So here is the main thing I want readers to learn about managing expectations in your quest to build a team: when I interview prospective agents I want to make sure they are the right fit in the ways that are most important to the success of my team. I want to make sure that they have an outgoing, "driver" personality. When I hire, I want men and women who want to storm the beach because this is a sales-driven business.

I use three criteria to hire future superstar agents and I encourage you to do the same.

1. **Are they reasonably likeable?** You are going to be spending a lot of time with them, and people who rub you wrong might be able to sell a house, but they will detract from the overall camaraderie of the office and the team, which will damage the all-important momentum and possibly drive other agents away. So if I don't personally have a good feeling about them, they don't get in (even if they come highly recommended).

2. **Do I trust them?** Teams are built on trust. You have to know that they will do what's right over what's best for them, even when it's hard. There's a lot of personal information flying around a busy real estate office (unfortunately, some gossip as well). You need to trust that they will pass along the information that is *supposed* to be passed along and, conversely, that they will be discreet when discretion is required.

3. **Do they have a "High ID" personality?** This is where science meets human nature. "High I" means "influential." "High D" means "driven." I go over them in more detail in Chapter 6, "Leveraging Yourself with Staff." But DISC assessments are an important part of my hiring process with both staff and with agents. Although I believe I am a perceptive person, I can't see into the future. DISC assessments are a simple but also *incredibly effective* aptitude test that can tell you if your potential new hire has the personality, drive, and ability to sell at a high level and become a high-octane superstar. DISC assessments are worth their weight in gold, and I never hire anyone — agent or assistant — without first administering one.

As for personality traits, the agents I hire have to be "sanguine." I love that word. They have to be friendly and able to connect. Sanguine means "cheerfully optimistic." People who are sanguine are truly fond of other people. So a personality balance between being a beach-stormer and being sanguine is what I'm looking for (more on that later in the chapter), and a simple DISC assessment will quickly bear this out in an applicant.

As I said earlier, consistency of personnel is another key to building a successful team. You've got to keep good agents in place.

Remember those great Pittsburgh Steelers football teams of the 1970s? No? Well, you were either too young or you aren't a football fan. How about the 1980s 49ers and Cowboys? Still no? *Really?* Well, you'll have to take my word for it then. The hallmark of those great football teams was consistent personnel. They had virtually the same talented teams for years, and the results were Super Bowl Championships.

One of the most important things I can tell you is that I don't want to train my agents for one to two years and then have them leave just as they are ready to put to use the knowledge I have given them. You don't want a revolving door! Consistency is an integral component of success. Experienced agents have two benefits. First, they know what's expected and can utilize the lessons you've taught them to sell homes and be successful. Second, experienced agents help you train the newcomers. So I tell all my prospective agents, right in the first interview, that I expect them to be a member of my team for four years. I tell them that I am going to take two years and train them. In those two years I give them everything I have and they get a level of training that they would be hard pressed to find anyplace else.

That's a pretty simple contract. But a four-year commitment encourages teamwork and camaraderie, while it has the *added* effect of making agents feel secure enough to grow and set down emotional and physical roots. The positive effect on the psyche of a team member who makes a four-year commitment cannot be overstated. In my agent agreements I give my new team members something more powerful and more binding than legalese. I give them the opportunity to live up to their word, as I will live up to mine.

So how do I live up to my part of the bargain? I have written into my agreements a stipulation that *very simply* says that if I, Brent Gove, *ever* do anything unethical, or ever do anything that lacks integrity (it's that vague and that broad) then that agent is absolutely free to leave me at any time and without repercussion.

This is not a loophole or an empty promise. There are no tricks, veiled threats, or hidden clauses. In fact, I take it a step further. I don't define "unethical" or "integrity" for my agents. I don't stipulate that they have to prove a thing. They are the judge and jury. And this helps them feel comfortable enough to make a four-year commitment because they know that, if they have to, or need to, they actually can leave. We both sign it. We both take a copy. And I've found that *much more* than any legal term or binding statement, it's the comprehensive training, it's the opportunity I deliver, and it's *our word* along with a clear understanding of what's expected that keeps my agents loyal. And then tell the prospective agent to take a week, talk it over with their family, and think about it. We end our meetings with a simple handshake because I believe that deep down just about everyone knows what's right and what's wrong.

So long as you make your expectations clear, and so long as you do everything you say you will do, you can still create a work environment based almost *entirely* on integrity. No legal contract on earth can make someone loyal. But expectation and clarity and follow-through can move mountains. Explain things clearly, and then shake their hand and look them in the eye. I think you'll find that no contract on earth is nearly as binding as that one.

So why have an agreement at all?

I have them sign because we all know that commitments in

THE BRENT GOVE REAL ESTATE GROUP

Mentoring Program Agreement

Team Member hereby makes a commitment to work with the Brent Gove Real Estate Group and **Brent Gove** for a period of 4 years. If Brent Gove does something un-ethical or that lacks integrity, **Team Member** is free to leave at that time.

Agent realizes Brent Gove will not be providing leads, but rather teaching you how to have a successful real estate business.

We look forward to assisting you.

_____   _____
, Team Member   Date

_____   _____
Brent T. Gove, Team Leader   Date

The Brent Gove Real Estate Group
Keller Williams Realty
3001 Lava Ridge Ct. Suite 100, Roseville, CA 95661
_916.480-8147   916.960-1871_

This is a sample of the four-year contract that agents and I sign.

real estate need to be in writing to preserve clarity *just in case.* When you don't follow that simple rule, trouble is going to find you. Of course you can't make a person loyal, but you can earn loyalty. I want them with me for four years, and the trade-off is that I am going to teach them to make a lot of money over the course of their lifetimes. I realize that a conversation about staying for four years could someday be forgotten. But a conversation, plus a week of deliberation and contemplation, plus a written agreement, plus intensive training, plus looking them in the eye and shaking their hands in agreement and understanding, *this* is the foundation of consistency on my team for everyone involved. And it works.

There is yet another advantage to thinking the decision through so carefully: People who are committed to something tend to do more to make it work. It's the difference between living together and entering into marriage. Does everyone who works with me love me? I hope so. But that's probably not the case. I'm intense. I'm driven. But I also like to have fun. I golf almost every Friday. My agents and I have been to Hawaii many times, and I truly like and appreciate them. And the reason for this mutual respect is that, first, I do what I say I am going to do. Second, I'm honest. Third, I honestly want them to succeed. Yes, it makes me money. But it thrills me, *absolutely thrills me,* when an agent that I have trained learns the business and becomes successful. Many of my former agents have gone on to build their own teams and have become fabulously wealthy and successful. And we are still friends. That bond of training and success lasts forever. That relationship — mentor and student and teammate — is, outside of family, one of the best relationships there is. It's incredibly rewarding.

Business Mistakes Happen — Go Easy

One of the biggest errors I see lead agents make is when they are too hard-line with their agents and staff. This seems to occur most often with their new hires. The new agent makes a mistake on a deal that will cost $1,400 to fix. But then the circumstances are compounded 1,000% because the shortsighted lead agent tells his new team member, "You're paying for that. I hope you learned a valuable lesson."

Ouch!

Here's what I know: If I'm the captain *and* the quarterback of the football team, and one of the lineman jumps offside and gets a five-yard penalty, is that lineman the only person who has to go back five yards? Of course not! We are a team. We all have to go back five yards and try again. And so this is an important point in managing agents and staff. I point out to my agent that he made a mistake and remind him or her that we all make mistakes. As a struggling, inexperienced agent with a million things to learn and remember, there is nothing, and I mean NOTHING, worse than trying your best, making a sale, feeling like you did a good job, and somehow something slips through and *wham!* You're hit with a bill for $1,400, and to compound matters, the lead agent takes it out of your check. Going backwards is not fun. You split the commission, so split the mistakes. Partner with them in their successes and their failures.

Conversely, lead agents who operate under the banner of "*You* messed up, *you pay*" do not create any loyalty. Why would they? I've seen it again and again with "High D" personality team leaders. You're not being tough-minded or disciplined. If you take money from your agents just because you can, then six months later, 12 months later, the person who is getting dinged right and left will feel no loyalty toward you and they'll be gone.

I love history. There are so many remarkable scenes in the HBO film series *Band of Brothers*. Although it's hard to choose any one scene that is the most inspirational, there is one particular conversation that takes place on the base in England as Easy Company prepares for D-Day, the great invasion to free Europe from the Nazis. The actors who play real-life heroes

Captain Dick Winters (who passed away this year on January 2, 2011, at the age of 92) and one of his new lieutenants, Lynn "Buck" Compton (who, as the lead prosecutor for the City of Los Angeles in 1968, helped convict Sirhan Sirhan, the man who killed Senator Robert F. Kennedy), are riding in a Jeep. It's only hours before the biggest invasion in the history of the world. The weather is overcast and the mood is serious as the magnitude *and the incredible danger* of what lies before them is foremost on every man's mind. Buck, an officer who is new to the unit, has been playing poker with some of the enlisted men, privates and corporals — he's proved the better player and has won their money — and Captain Winters is concerned. He's questioning the wisdom of Buck having gambled with the men. He tells Buck that he doesn't want him to gamble with them ever again.

Buck's a good man (and besides being a famous Los Angeles prosecutor, Buck Compton is also in the UCLA Baseball Hall of Fame), but he doesn't understand what the problem is. "What's the big deal?" he asks.

Winters replies, "I don't want you to ever be in a position to take from these men."

That's leadership. And as I remember the scene, it gives me chills.

Now, of course I'm not comparing the incredible heroism of those World War II D-Day veterans with my agents and me splitting the cost of a mistake. But I do mention it for motivation and for reflection. I am 100% serious that you want to make certain that you split those mistakes with your agents, because you are a team. Your agents are out there to make you *and themselves* money. They are out there trying to make a living to feed their families. Fairness and good feelings will earn you loyalty and help to build a team whose members watch each other's backs.

We are a team, so the agent is never hung out to dry. Don't ever send a new agent home to face their spouse $1,400 poorer than when the day began. Sometimes I pay for the error, but most of the time I split it with them (or, for more experienced

rs, divide the amount according to the commis-
, be it 50/50 or 60/40 or 70/30). Most agents, if
_..y make a mistake, actually *want* to take responsibility for
the error. If they are going to make me money, then *that* river
doesn't flow just one way. This, splitting
the cost of mistakes, helps to form a bond
— it gives us something to laugh about (or
at least learn from) — and it makes us a
team. Besides, it's good business and good
manners. So, expenses, by and large, and
mistakes, are split between the agent and me. And I believe that
anyone building a team should realize the value, and the fairness,
in splitting expenses incurred by mistakes. This way, instead of a
$1,400 dollar mistake, it's a $700 mistake. They will appreciate
you for it and they will absolutely do better the next time around.

> Don't ever send a new agent home to face their spouse $1,400 poorer than when the day began.

So, first: a four-year commitment. Second: every mistake is
a 50/50 split. We're a team and we all win or we all lose. Third:
have a written commission plan.

Commission Structures of Team Members

The first year I partner with an agent it's a 50/50 commission
split. I realize the word "partner" can be thrown around pretty
casually, but when I use it I mean it, because the agent does
not work *for* me. Not in any traditional or strict sense. When
someone works for you, they do a job and you pay them for
it, which is absolutely not what we do in real estate. We work
together to create a profit in the form of commissions. And we
split that commission as any partnership would, right down
the middle, 50/50.

The second year, I tilt the partnership in their favor with a
60/40 split. The reason for the shift is both simple and straightforward: they need me less in the second year.

Obviously, if I've done my job, the agent hardly needs me

at all in their third year. I reward them for their commitment with a 70/30 split. They get 70% of the profit and I get 30%.

The fourth year we proceed to an 80/20 split, which I am proud to be a part of. The only caveat is that if the lead is generated by my office, I take a 20% referral fee to help offset the costs of things like staff and advertising.

As for the first year with a newly hired agent, some lead agents feel guilty about asking for 50%, but I don't. We are partners. My firm, my knowledge, my referrals, all these facets and years of work evolve to become *our knowledge* and *our business*. And if you are truly providing the foundations for success for your new agents — *truly and honestly* teaching — then you are mentoring and preparing them for a long and lucrative career, giving them insider knowledge that is going to serve them throughout their lives. If that is *truly and honestly* the case, then 50% is fair, because what you provide is invaluable to them, it's rewarding to you, and it should serve both parties for a long, long time.

I do know agents who start their new hires off at 70/30 because, certainly, there are places out there where even a novice agent can do better than a 50/50 split. But I work very hard to assure my new partners that there is no place where they will receive the powerful hands-on training that we provide. And my experience has been that lead agents who hire at 70/30 give very little training in return. It's no coincidence that with that type of hands-off style new agents may flounder for several years. They may even have to start all over again with a new team that actually trains them because the intention of the hands-off lead agent to create a lasting team probably just isn't there.

However, you've got to *not only believe, but* KNOW *in your heart* that you will work harder for your partners than anyone else. You must understand that their success is — in every way — *your* success. If you do not believe this, you will have problems *attracting and keeping* top talent. If you do not truly feel in your heart that you are looking out for the best interests of your team, you will not get the talented, quality agents to join you — and those are the agents you need most! It's simple: the better the agents you attract, the more successful you will be.

My agents know I expect a four-year commitment. I make it clear that they will get more training from me than any other firm out there. I stand by that. My new team members know about the 50/50, 60/40, 70/30 and 80/20 splits. They understand that I pay the staff, the rent, the lease, the phones, the housekeeper, the fax and copier, and because I do those things they don't have to worry about doing anything but learning and selling.

One more thing: *I do not ever renegotiate the commission structure.* I put that in writing and I *not only* have them sign the agreement, we read through it together. I have friends at other firms who mention to me that agents are constantly coming up to them attempting to renegotiate their splits. That's usually the lead agent's fault because they probably never clearly defined the partnership terms up-front. Some agents just shoot from the hip. But sooner or later, disorganized, wishful-thinking lead agents get outgunned.

> **I do not ever renegotiate the commission structure.**

So, get the agreement in writing. But just as important, make it a ceremony and *read the agreement* TOGETHER.

How Do You Find the Right Partner Agents for Your Team?

I *highly* recommend that you DISC-assess every potential hire. The DISC assessment is a behavioral assessment tool that provides feedback for building on strengths and increasing personal effectiveness. DISC is an acronym for Dominance, Influence, Steadiness, and Conscientiousness. People who take them will be classified as one of those four categories being their key or dominant personality characteristic. The assessment further identifies personality types by listing a secondary characteristic that, when combined with the first, predicts behavior.

Now, for the record, there isn't one combination of traits that doesn't have numerous professional strengths and aptitudes for success. I can't emphasize this enough: it's not about good or bad, smart or dumb, right or wrong. It's about sales aptitude. *Big ticket* real estate sales, which is vastly different from cars or appliances or investments. So, for the purposes and goals of *Momentum,* we'll talk about how DISC assessments influence whom I hire as agents, who I don't, and why.

> **I highly recommend that you DISC-assess every potential hire.**

Again, if someone tests, say, primary S (steadiness) and secondary C (conscientiousness) rather than primary D or primary I, I don't hire them. Primary S and secondary C are the complete opposite of what I look for in an agent, and while they may be great, amazing, interesting people — your spouse, or a college president, even — we are in the people business, and this business demands that you have above-average people skills.

My personal favorite hire is an ID. An I is a life-of-the-party type. They want to hug you when they see you. They want to have you over to a barbecue. They are great with the public and can connect to people quickly. They tend to want to make money and expect to have fun doing it. (Companies that offer DISC assessments are very good at explaining what they do and how they do it. You'll pick up on the jargon and the traits of what you are looking for in agents in no time.)

The D is the second trait IDs are known for. The personality type of I is outgoing and optimistic, and the personality trait of D is driven. So when the chips are down, IDs typically want to go out and work 14 hours a day and make money and fix it. Rain, snow, sleet, hail, recession, depression, 104 degrees outside, the Yankees in last place, they won't be stopped and don't cower behind obstacles waiting for the storm to pass. IDs would have been great riders for the Pony Express. They will not be defeated because they are both optimistic *and* outgoing. They will succeed because they are driven. So, my preference is to lead-hire the I and the D in that order. It seems to work best for me. And my strong recommendation would be to hire only IDs as agents.

Now, DIs naturally will say, "Hey, what about us?" My response is to tell you that high DIs are some of the most powerful people on earth. They enter politics and don't just run companies, they run countries. They are often great CEOs and entrepreneurs, and *lots* of successful realtors are high DIs.

However, DIs can be trouble as buyer's agents or partner-agents. It's very much like a Western where the two gunslingers immediately decide that the town ain't big enough for the both of them. DIs may question you at every turn and are motivated, not just to succeed, but to dominate, to take over, even, because they are natural conquerors. DIs also have a tendency to burn their bridges and go for broke. It's simply how a large percentage of them were designed by God and then nurtured by mom and dad.

I've hired almost every combination possible on the DISC test. But in all that time only IDs have managed to start fast and keep going. I've had more than one who sold seven houses in her very first month in the business. And, with a few exceptions, the agents I've worked with who have not only started lightning fast but also continued on for many years at a super-high rate of speed have also been IDs.

Training: When and How Often

I don't formally hold training sessions on Mondays. Informally, the teaching never stops. But officially, I don't schedule training seminars or classes on Mondays because everyone is slammed coming out of the weekend; Manic Mondays are actually my favorite day in the office. It's like Christmas morning! Exciting things happen each and every Monday and that makes them special days. I've come to the office anticipating maybe five or six deals, and actually had 25 sitting on my desk. There's nothing else in real estate that compares. And if you are netting $2,000 on each of those deals? That's not only loads of fun, but it's the kind of math that just about *anyone* can do. Mondays like those actually make you wish that the weekends would go by faster.

But those kinds of Mondays don't happen without training. They only happen with weeks, even years, of consistent exchanges of information followed by equally consistent reinforcement. With long-term success as the goal, and with training the foundation of that success, I long ago realized that the timing of my training is almost as important as the content. *When* to train? That's as important as it is easy. Simply, when are members of my team *most receptive* to the lessons I want to teach?

I avoid Friday training almost entirely (unless there's a once-in-a-lifetime speaker who just can't be there any other day). There are more absences on Fridays than any other day of the week. In fact, I'm as likely to be out enjoying myself on a Friday as any other day. It's really pretty simple: people take trips that start Thursday night.

> The timing of my training is almost as important as the content.

Or maybe they've had a good week and they might want to celebrate. A bad week? And maybe they just need a break. And because in our profession, weekends are prime working hours, I recommend my agents take Fridays off so that then they can slay the dragon over the weekend.

Which brings to mind the art of pacing. Naturally, in sales you need to strike while the iron is hot. For some, that means putting in long days and long weeks. I recommend that my agents, no matter how hot they are, take at least one day off every week. Now, some people are reading this and saying, "Only one day, is he kidding?" while others are reading it and thinking, "I'm building my business and the market is hot (or cold)! Can I really afford to take a day off?"

At the beginning of a career there is a tendency to overwork and overschedule. But I say, don't be a real estate ninja! Working seven days a week in the beginning, middle, or end of your career is absolutely foolish! It will hurt your health, your family, and, inevitably, destroy all your hard work one stressed-out minute at a time. I monitor overwork with my agents just as I do with myself. And while I work hard, I don't work foolishly. We are not made to work every minute of every day. Working seven days a week is a recipe for burnout, and worse, it's a guarantee of a disastrous personal life at home.

So with Mondays and Fridays out, I'm a big believer in training that takes place Tuesday, Wednesday, or Thursday. Those days have the highest rates of attendance, the highest rates of retention, and they provide agents and trainees with the most opportunities to put what has been taught into action right away. After 14 years, my *every week* training time — the time that, barring an unusual event, I'm most likely to conduct training that is *not* to be missed by my agents — is 10:00 to 11:00 every Tuesday morning.

> I'm a big believer in training that takes place Tuesday, Wednesday, or Thursday.

I'm often asked by other lead agents:"What do you talk about in all those meetings?"

Here's a small sampling of ideas for two months' worth of Tuesday training sessions:

Week one: Lead generation.

Week two: Follow-up.

Week three: Internet marketing (I love to have an Internet magician come in and dazzle my staff with website optimization or lead generation such as pay-per-click, etc.).

Week four: Ways to get listings.

Week five: Database.

Week six: Disclosures.

Week seven: Legal matters. How to avoid getting sued.

Week eight: I'll have a guest speaker. Maybe last year's rookie of the year. Let them share their stories. Let them share their "Aha!" moments.

Be creative. Try having your favorite mortgage broker come educate you and your team on the latest loan programs. Have your home inspector give advice. Your general contractor. The agent who made five sales last week. The list of possibilities is endless! Thirty minutes with a yellow notepad and you have your team meetings laid out for a year.

If every day can't be "Commission Monday," then I wish every day could be "Training Tuesday." That is one of the most exciting days in my office. My meetings are not lectures, but very loose and freewheeling. We learn, but more than that, we exchange ideas and ask questions. There's a lot of bonding, but there's also always a lot of learning that goes beyond the topic of that particular day's training session.

Incentives to Assist Your Team in Helping You

One of the ways to attract, motivate, and *keep* a top-notch team together is by using incentives. Let's begin with agents: Let's say I offer incentives that are to be earned over a seven-month period. I say, "Sell 14 homes in a seven-month period and I'll send you to the Caribbean." Well, 14 homes in seven months equals two homes per month — 24 homes in a year. What if you have 10 agents and they all earn the incentive?

I've taken as many as 120 people (agents, staff, and families) to Maui and stayed at the Sheraton Black Rock — which is not a cheap place. But when you buy that many tickets and book that many rooms, you get incredible discounts that equal wholesale rates. Not long ago I could get seven nights in Maui for two people (per couple) for $1,500 — which included airfare. Now this may sound expensive. And the idea of laying out $50,000 may seem like a long way off to you, but I *clearly* remember how badly I once wanted to make $50,000 in a single year!

Build your business the right way from the ground-up and that level of success can be yours.

But this is not about vacation, it's about the perks that enable you to *hire and keep* really good agents for longer than the amount of time it takes to train them. Because I have found that *serious* vacations, blow-out stays in Maui or the Bahamas, these perks, which can be first-class but also affordable, are worth a lot more than just cash bonuses. They create *lasting* bonds. They give agents something to look forward to. And competing for trips creates a positive buzz around the office. When you compete for trips that everyone can enjoy *together*, I've noticed that the agents seem to pull for one another much more (more than, say, cash bonuses) because they want everyone to be able to go and have a great time. In contrast, money is very personal, while trips are communal. Money comes in and is gone. The good feeling of taking or winning a trip lasts forever. And I can't tell you how many times I've been on trips with my team, and someone's spouse will come up to me and say, "This is our first vacation in nine years."

That's one of the pleasures of building a team of agents. Working together and then enjoying the fruits of that labor.

Be successful. Earn their trust, train them well, do what you promise, and you can assemble *and maintain* a team that *not only* makes you money, but sets that agent up for a successful and rewarding career.

I promise you that there is virtually nothing you will ever accomplish in our business that will feel better than that!

For interviews, to hire Brent Gove to speak at your event,
to order his books or DVDs, or to get a schedule of Brent's seminar
dates and locations, contact Brent's office at
BrentGoveSeminars.com or 916-223-5555

Brent has a newsletter! For more information, go to:
www.BrentGove.com or www.BrentGoveSeminars.com

To purchase *Momentum: A Strategic Guide to Success
for Real Estate Agents and Brokers*
go to www.IrishCanonPress.com
or email info@irishcanonpress.com

Momentum is available wherever books are sold.

For bulk discounts, contact Irish Canon Press.

Brent is on Twitter: GoveMomentum

Follow Brent, Momentum, and Irish Canon Press on Facebook